REGIONAL ARCHAEOLOGIES · EAST ANGLIA

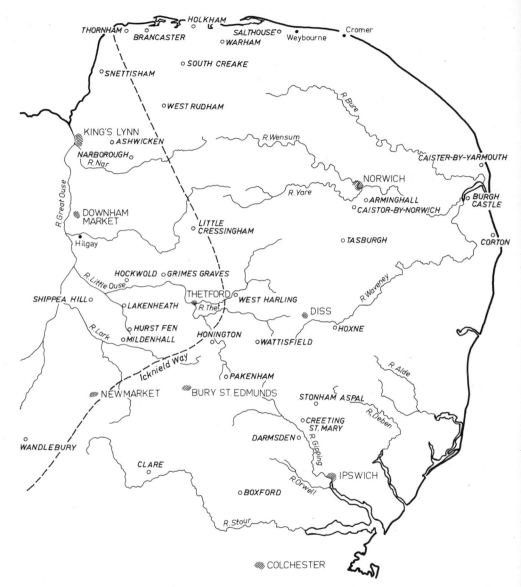

Fig. 1 *East Anglia, showing sites mentioned in the text*

REGIONAL ARCHAEOLOGIES

East Anglia

BY HELEN CLARKE

HEINEMANN EDUCATIONAL BOOKS · LONDON

Regional Archaeologies

GENERAL EDITOR: D. M. WILSON, M.A., F.S.A.
Reader in Archaeology of the Anglo-Saxon Period at the University of London

Heinemann Educational Books Ltd
LONDON   EDINBURGH   MELBOURNE   TORONTO
AUCKLAND   SINGAPORE   JOHANNESBURG
HONG KONG   NAIROBI   IBADAN   NEW DELHI

ISBN 0 435 32972 3

Published by Heinemann Educational Books Ltd
48 Charles Street, London W1X 8AH
Photoset in Malta by St. Paul's Press Ltd
Printed in Great Britain by Morrison and Gibb
London and Edinburgh

Contents

List of Illustrations

Acknowledgements

The author is most grateful to all those who have so kindly helped in the preparation of this book, especially to Miss A. S. Mottram of King's Lynn Museum and Art Gallery who has provided both study space and encouragement over many years. Photographic material has been obtained from Norwich Castle Museum, Ipswich Museum, The British Museum, the Ministry of Public Building and Works and the Committee for Aerial Photography, University of Cambridge; the line drawings were prepared by Mrs. Eva Wilson. Many thanks are also due to the editors of the series for their many helpful suggestions, particularly on textual matters, but the greatest thanks of all must be reserved for the author's husband for his constant and invaluable assistance, advice and criticism.

Copyright is held in the photographs used in this book as follows: British Museum, figs. 28, 30, 31, 32, 35, 36; Norwich Castle Museum, figs. 22, 27, 34, 43; Ipswich Museum, fig. 37; J. K. S. St. Joseph, fig. 40; Ministry of Public Building and Works, figs. 42.

1 The Countryside Before Man

East Anglia, comprising the present counties of Norfolk, Suffolk and the eastern fringes of the Cambridgeshire fenland, has always been an isolated area of Britain, surrounded as it is by the sea to the north and east, the fens to the west and the heavy clay lowlands of Essex (thickly wooded until modern times) to the south. Its only easily traversable physical link with central and southern England is the chalk ridge, joining with the Chilterns at the region's south-west boundary, along which runs the Icknield Way, a prehistoric trackway later converted into a Roman road. For these reasons, contacts between East Anglia and the rest of England have often been tenuous and we shall see how, throughout the prehistoric and Roman period, the cultural development of the region owed almost as much to influences which travelled across the North Sea from the Low Countries and adjacent areas of the Continent as to those from the rest of England. East Anglian life and traditions, therefore, have always been a curious blend of English and continental traits developed within East Anglian isolation and giving the area a distinctive character of its own.

THE GEOLOGICAL BACKGROUND

The gently rolling countryside, nowhere reaching a height greater than 300 feet above sea level, reflects an underlying solid geology of comparative simplicity, but the surface deposits are very much more complex as a result of the four glaciations which affected the area. East Anglia is the youngest part of the British Isles and its basic structure represents the most recent periods of rock formation, with the oldest strata laid down only 150 million years ago in the Jurassic age. The various strata representing the Jurassic and later deposits run roughly north to south across the counties, the oldest in the west, and become progressively more recent as they approach the east coast (fig. 2).

The earliest deposit is the Kimmeridge Clay which outcrops at various places from Hilgay in south-west Norfolk to just north of King's Lynn; this stiff, bluish-grey clay is very rich in fossils, particularly of fish and marine reptiles. Overlying the Kimmeridge Clay to the east is the Lower Greensand belt which extends roughly from Downham Market northwards to Hunstanton and contains such varied materials as the fine-grained Sandringham Sands, the iron-bearing Carstone, and Gault Clay.

Yet further eastwards and forming the basis of the central part of the region, commonly known as High Norfolk and High Suffolk, lies the chalk. This, the dominant feature of the whole of East Anglia, is entirely of marine origin and in places is 1350 feet thick. It outcrops occasionally in the west and the north-west but is covered in the east by more recent deposits. The chalk contains many rich seams of flint which have been

9

exploited throughout man's history for the manufacture of tools and weapons and even, in medieval and modern times, for building material.

In the remaining part of the region, east of a line from Weybourne to Diss, the main geological formations are the Crag deposits which overlie the eastern edge of the chalk. The Crags—Norwich, Red and Weybourne—which are shelly sands mixed with clay and gravel, were laid down in a period when the land was submerged under a precursor of the present North Sea. They were formed during the change from the Pliocene to Pleistocene era when there was a progressive lowering of temperatures, culminating in the great glaciations. There is evidence for the beginning of the Ice Age in East Anglia in the Weybourne Crag where there are fossil remains of animals which can be recognized as belonging to present-day arctic areas.

ICE AGE AND RECENT DEPOSITS

Covering this fairly simple basic structure is the much more complex pattern of the drift deposits, that is, the various soils which cover the underlying rock and largely dictate the present vegetation and land usage. The accumulation of these soils was the result of material being transported and released by the four ice sheets which covered the region either wholly or partially. In highly simplified terms, East Anglian surface deposits consist of two main types. Firstly, there is a Chalky Boulder Clay which lies over the chalk and forms the soils of High Norfolk and High Suffolk. Today this soil is very fertile, but it was too heavy for cultivation by prehistoric man. Secondly, to both east and west of the high lands lie areas of lighter soils—mainly sands and

gravels—which support heath vegetation in places such as the Greensand Belt of north-west Norfolk, the Sandlings area of south-east Suffolk and the breckland (fig. 2) (where sands overlying chalk form the nearest approach to steppeland in Britain). We shall see in later chapters how some East Anglian areas were more favourable to prehistoric settlement than others; generally it seems that prehistoric man found the most suitable conditions in the breckland and Sandling regions which were both lightly wooded heathlands supporting birch and hazel scrub. Often they have formed two distinct population centres separated by the uninhabited Chalky Boulder Clay which was clothed with heavy oak forests forming a barrier to communication between east and west.

More recent soil types are represented on the north Norfolk coast and in fenland. The northern coastline shows much evidence for post-glacial variation and even today it is constantly being changed by the formation of salt marshes. The fenland, which lies on the western edge of the region, has been formed in post-glacial times by subsidence and flooding with sea water which deposited silt in the north; and in the south by fresh-water flooding which allowed the build-up of peat. Today, the fenland is one of the most fertile areas of Britain, but it has only become so through drainage; in its natural very wet and marshy state the fenland acted as a barrier between East Anglia and the rest of England. It was not until the Roman period, when drainage began and the climate was drier, that occupation of the fenland became possible.

East Anglia is drained by a number of distinct river systems (fig. 1), the valleys

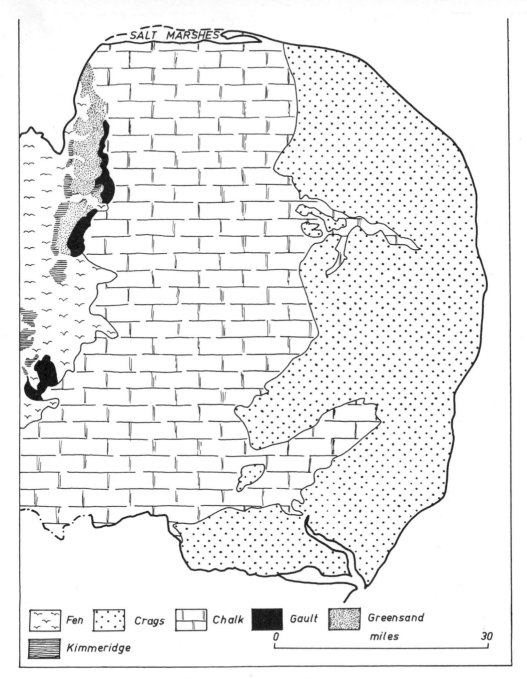

SALT MARSHES

Fen | Crags | Chalk | Gault | Greensand

Kimmeridge

0   30
miles

Fig. 2 *Solid geology of East Anglia*

11

of which served as a means of communication in the prehistoric period. On the east coast the Bure, Yare and Wensum flow into the North Sea at Yarmouth while in south-east Suffolk the estuaries of the Stour, Orwell, Gipping and Deben form another system. The River Great Ouse, which flows northwards through the fens, has a number of tributaries and of these the Lark and Little Ouse drain north-west Suffolk and the Nar and Wissey west Norfolk. The Waveney, flowing eastwards to join the North Sea at Yarmouth, forms part of the present boundary between the two counties.

Contacts between east and west could most easily be achieved by travelling along the Gipping and Little Ouse or along the Stour and Lark valleys which formed a link between the two most populous areas of prehistoric times— the breckland and the Ipswich region. Further north, contact between east and west Norfolk could best be maintained through the Little Ouse and the Waveney valley. It was therefore possible for prehistoric man to travel across East Anglia, but the routes were by no means easy with the result that the easterly and westerly parts of the region tended to develop in isolation.

2 The Arrival of Man in East Anglia: The Palaeolithic

During the Ice Age, East Anglia, although affected by a succession of great ice sheets, was not subjected to continuous arctic conditions. When the ice retreated during the so-called *inter-glacials,* the temperature was higher and the climate allowed the development of a relatively rich vegetation. Following the plants came animals, and in their wake came man (see Table 1).

The cold period began over 500,000 years ago with a progressive deterioration of the climate. It was at this time that the arctic animals whose fossils have been found in the Crag deposits of eastern East Anglia lived in the region.

The final deposition of Crag material at Weybourne in north Norfolk contains nothing but arctic species—a reflection of the climate at the time of the first glaciation. Three other cold phases, known as the Lowestoft, Gipping and Weichselian glaciations (Table 1), followed. The ice-free periods which separate these—the Cromer, Hoxne and Ipswichian interglacials—are periods when the glaciers withdrew, leaving behind a vast spread of outwash deposits which were mentioned in the last chapter. They also left behind a climate suitable for human settlement. There were some other withdrawals of the ice known

Table 1 *Chronology of Glacial Periods*

Date B.C.	Climate			Geology	Archaeology
	East Anglian	N.W. European	Swiss		
10,000	Post-glacial	Post-glacial	Post-glacial	North Norfolk Coast and Fens	Arrival of Mesolithic hunters
15,000	Post-glacial	Post-glacial	Post-glacial	North Norfolk Coast and Fens	Final withdrawal of the ice
	Last or Weichselian Glaciation	Weichselian Glaciation	Würm Glaciation	Hunstanton Till Drop in sea level Land bridge	No evidence of human occupation of East Anglia Elsewhere, Upper and Middle Palaeolithic *Homo sapiens*
200,000					
	Last or Ipswichian Interglacial	Eemian Interglacial	Riss-Würm Interglacial	Rise in sea level First formation of English Channel	Lower Palaeolithic Acheulian and Levalloisian cultures
300,000	Gipping Glaciation	Saale Glaciation	Riss Glaciation	Gipping Till and gravels	Levalloisian culture arrived during Interstadial
	Hoxnian Interglacial	Hoxnian Interglacial	Mindel-Riss Interglacial	Hoxne Lake deposits	Acheulian culture *Neanderthal* man
400,000	Lowestoft Glaciation	Elster Glaciation	Mindel Glaciation	Lowestoft Till	Man, *Homo erectus*, first arrived in an Interstadial, bringing Clactonian culture
	Cromerian Interglacial	Cromerian Interglacial	Günz-Mindel Interglacial	Cromer Forest beds	Eoliths
500,000	First or Baventian Glaciation	Günz Glaciation		Crag deposits	Eoliths

as *interstadials*, but these were of lesser extent and occurred within the major glaciations themselves.

Man first appears to have arrived in Britain about 400,000 years ago during an interstadial of the Lowestoft glaciation. One of the results of the advance and retreat of the ice caps was a fluctuation in sea level which eventually, during the Ipswichian interglacial (about 200,000 years ago), was sufficient to form the English Channel. Subsequently, during the Weichselian glaciation, the sea level dropped again and a land bridge was formed between Britain and Europe. This existed until about 5000 B.C. when the steady rise in sea level, caused by the melting of the ice sheet, resulted in Britain finally becoming severed from Europe.

Fig. 3 *Eoliths from Bramford (left) and Foxhall, Suffolk*

Lower Palaeolithic hunters reached Britain from the east before this separation took place. They brought with them a distinctive tool-making culture which has left considerable remains. Deliberately shaped stone tools made by these people provide the only evidence for the existence of early man in East Anglia. The ability to shape stone, and particularly flint, into tools which conform to a regular pattern appears to have been one of the first things to set man apart from the rest of the animal kingdom, and this has given rise to the definition of man as a tool-making animal.

The significance of tools was first realized in 1797 when the antiquarian John Frere suggested that some stone objects found at Hoxne in Suffolk represented implements belonging 'to a very remote period indeed; even beyond that of the present world'. These observations sparked off great interest in the early history of man in East Anglia and since that time the region has been one of the most important in the study of Palaeolithic man in Britain. The area is particularly favourable for this research because of its well-established succession of glacials and interglacials, and

also because of the high quality of the flint found in the great chalk cap of central Norfolk and Suffolk. This material, with its smooth, even texture and its ability to form a sharp cutting edge, was ideal for tool-making and was used extensively not only by Palaeolithic man but also by men of subsequent ages, and it formed the basis of East Anglia's wealth in the Late Neolithic Age.

EOLITHS

Although it is generally believed today that man did not appear in Britain until sometime during the Lowestoft or second glaciation there has been a great deal of controversy in the past about the possibility of man's presence in East Anglia even earlier than this—at a time when the Crag deposits were being laid down in the east of the region. The basis for this belief is the existence of so-called *eoliths* (literally: 'stones from the dawn of time') which have been found at the base and at higher levels in the Red Crag deposits in Suffolk, at the base of the Norwich Crag and in the Cromer Forest Bed.

These eoliths consist of flints which in many ways resemble the flake, core and

14

hand-axe shapes of Palaeolithic tools which can be seen in fig. 4. Eoliths (fig. 3) often display a quite convincing flake technique and occasionally even secondary retouching (the trimming of a flake by the removal of smaller flakes to give a sharp, serviceable edge) which is normally considered one of the criteria for distinguishing man-made tools from natural unworked stones. In some cases the eolith flints are fresh, as if unused, while others are abraded or rolled as a result of having been transported with glacial deposits; both of these features are also found in well-attested man-made palaeoliths.

Explanations for the production of eoliths have been sought in natural phenomena which could produce the percussion and pressure flaking of flints. Such things as the pressure and movement of glaciers, rivers flowing rapidly over stony beds, rock falls and the action of waves on storm beaches may all lead to the purely haphazard shaping of flints, and even to secondary retouching.

A rough guide to the requirements for a man-made tool would be that the object should conform to some regular pattern, that is, that a number of similar types or shapes made in an identical way might be found; that its shape should be the result of flaking from two or three directions at right angles to each other; and finally that it should be found associated with other signs of human activity such as other tools or the waste products from their manufacture. If all these requirements are met then it is fairly safe to assume that an object is man-made, but if any requirement is absent then the assumption is more rash.

As was mentioned earlier, the beginning of the Ice Age was accompanied

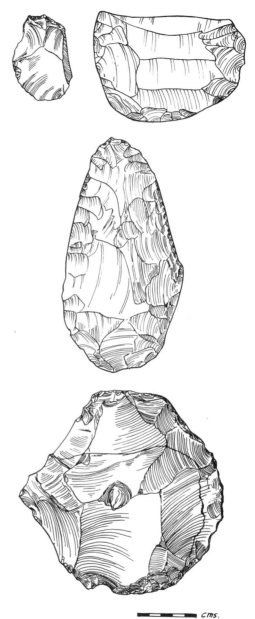

Fig. 4 *Clactonian flake from Clacton (top left); Aechulian scraper (top right) and hand-axe (centre) from Hoxne: Levalloisian tortoise core from Blundon*

Flint was worked to produce tools and weapons, and individual groups of people produced specific types of equipment to suit their own requirements. Both the method of making flint implements, and the groups of these implements or *assemblages*, are characteristics of the culture of their makers.

Throughout the whole of the Palaeolithic the remains that have been found show us that the culture and economy of the people changed very little. Hunting remained the basis of the economy and food was supplemented by wild berries and seeds, but cultivation of crops and domestication of animals were unknown. Communities, perhaps family groups, lived in temporary shelters or caves and presumably moved seasonally following game. In East Anglia much of the land was heavily wooded with mixed oak forest, and movements of population and settlements must have been restricted to the river valleys and terraces. If the places where flint implements have been found are plotted on a map, their distribution illustrates this (fig. 5).

Tools have been found from the Lower Palaeolithic in East Anglia in great numbers, but this is not necessarily an indication of a large population. Flint tools were only useful when freshly made; their sharp edges are brittle and easily blunted so they would need to be made in large quantities, especially when butchering after a kill. It is, therefore, not unusual to find literally dozens of hand-axes together, which may all have been made by a handful of people.

THE CLACTONIAN CULTURE

Man's first migration into East Anglia brought with it a distinctive method of flint working known as the Chopper-Core industry. The migrants practised the earliest and most primitive Palaeolithic flint technique, and once established in England their culture becomes known as the *Clactonian* culture, named from the site where the tools were first recognized, Clacton-on-Sea, Essex.

These hunters lived during the first half of the Hoxnian interglacial which followed the Lowestoft glaciation, between 300,000 and 400,000 years ago, and differed physically from modern man to such an extent that they are recognized as a separate species, *Homo erectus*. Their chopper-core implements are rudimentary axes or choppers formed by the rough trimming of pebbles to give a simple cutting edge (fig. 4). Flakes which result from this trimming were used for cutting and scraping without further modification, and this basic simplicity is the main characteristic of Clactonian technique although, at a later stage in development, flakes were more accurately shaped by secondary working.

The only site in East Anglia which has produced a large amount of material of this age is that at Barnham in Suffolk, on the banks of the Little Ouse, where men settled on gravels which merge into the outwash from the glaciers of the Lowestoft era.

THE ACHEULIAN CULTURE

Overlapping the Clactonian is the much better represented *Acheulian* culture, named after St. Acheul in France where the tool-types were first found. This culture may have lasted for about 300,000 years (from the Hoxnian to the Ipswichian interglacial) and is associated with *Neanderthal man* who reached Britain from Africa, perhaps via Spain and France. It is characterized by its principal tool, the flint hand-axe, which is a much more sophisticated version of the Clactonian chopper and shows definite signs of development throughout its very long history. Acheulian hand-axes fall basically into two types, pointed and ovate, and there are also a number of tools made from flint flakes which were used as scrapers and cleavers (fig. 4). These four types of tool suggest a hunting and food-gathering economy much more diversified than that of the Clactonians, whose needs were fulfilled by much simpler implements.

During the warm climate of the two interglacials the countryside was inhabited by animals such as elephant, hippopotamus, rhinoceros, lion and sabre-toothed tiger, all of which may have been the prey of the Acheulian hunters. We have little or no evidence of the dwellings of Acheulian man, but groups of Acheulian tools have been found at Hoxne, Mildenhall and at other Suffolk sites in lake mud deposits, and this suggests that the main areas of occupation were beside lakes and rivers.

THE LEVALLOISIAN CULTURE

The drop in temperature during the Gipping glaciation forced most of the hunters to withdraw to the south, but there does seem to have been slight occupation in East Anglia at this time, perhaps during an interstadial, and it was during this glacial period that the first tools belonging to the *Levalloisian* culture were made in the British Isles. The main difference between Acheulian and Levalloisian cultures is that the latter specialized in flake rather than core tools. Any necessary shaping of the flake was done before it was detached from the core, which was of a tortoise shape (with one side flat and the other convex). A single blow would strike off a ready-worked flake tool from this core. This technique appears to be a development from the Acheulian method, but it is quite different from the late Clactonian technique where flakes were struck off a core and reworked afterwards to make the correct shape. The site at Brundon in Suffolk has produced good evidence for this culture in East Anglia, and its general distribution is again along river valleys (fig. 5).

THE MIDDLE AND UPPER PALAEOLITHIC

It has been shown (p. 13) that during the Ipswichian interglacial the British Isles were cut off from Europe for the first time. This meant that Britain was no longer in physical contact with the centres of European Palaeolithic development and did not keep pace with the cultural and material developments on the Continent. Nothing in this country, for instance, approaches achievements such as the cave paintings of France and Spain and there is even a lack of innovation in British flint working.

From the end of the Ipswichian interglacial throughout the final, Weichselian, glaciation we have no firm evidence for human occupation in East Anglia. Although the ice of this glacier did not cover more than the north coast of Norfolk, the region was apparently uninhabited, whereas we know from other areas of Britain that groups of hunters were occupying the higher lands of the Pennines and the south-west, mainly living in caves and producing flint tools by the flake technique. In East Anglia, a few implements resembling Middle or Upper Palaeolithic types have been found, allegedly from the Boulder Clay laid down by the Weichselian glaciation, but it is generally accepted that these objects belong to the subsequent period, the Mesolithic, which will be dealt with in the following chapter.

The main historical significance of the Upper Palaeolithic period in the British Isles is that it saw the first occupation of the area by modern man, *Homo sapiens*.

3 The Final Withdrawal of the Ice: Mesolithic Hunters

Once the ice had finally retreated with the withdrawal of the last glaciation, perhaps somewhere about 10,000 years ago, man was able to establish himself permanently throughout the British Isles. During the Palaeolithic period man's settlement had been mainly confined to the lowland areas of Britain, but from the beginning of the *Mesolithic* period onwards he also lived in the highland areas of the north and west.

The Mesolithic period—Middle Stone Age—covers the time between the final withdrawal of the ice and the arrival in Britain of groups of people who brought with them a totally new culture and economy. These were the people of the Neolithic or New Stone Age whose livelihood was based on agriculture and who consequently developed more settled communities and a much more highly organized way of life. The Mesolithic people, however, had not yet developed such an economy; their main occupations were hunting, fishing and food-gathering in much the same way as

their Palaeolithic predecessors from whom they inherited many cultural traits and from whom is derived all the material equipment considered to be typical of the Mesolithic hunter-fisher.

The withdrawal of the ice sheet northwards was accompanied by a climatic improvement which led to a change from the tundra-like vegetation of the Upper Palaeolithic to mixed birch and pine woodland. The climate continued to improve over the succeeding millennia, birch was replaced by pine as the dominant plant, hazel became more common and elm and oak were established as important forest trees. Change in vegetation was accompanied by change in fauna, from the more cold-tolerant animals of the Upper Palaeolithic (reindeer, horse and bison) to the dominance of red and roe deer, cattle and pigs, while some horses still remained although in much smaller numbers.

The characteristic tools of the Mesolithic period are adaptations of the Palaeolithic flake implements to make them more suitable for use in hunting the changed fauna. The main tools now are composed of *microliths* (small flint flakes) which were hafted onto a wooden handle in a variety of different ways to form either arrows or saw-like cutting edges. In the main, tools of sufficient size to dismember large animals are missing, and this reflects the change in environment.

At some point during this period, probably about 5000 B.C., the rising sea level once again submerged part of what is now the North Sea and, by forming the present English Channel, cut the British Isles off from the Continent. This tended once more to isolate Britain from continental developments although cultural influences, now waterborne, continued to reach this country from Europe.

THE MAGLEMOSIANS

During the earlier part of the Mesolithic period, however, the British Isles were still physically connected to Europe by a land bridge (p. 13); this consisted of an area of marshland and lagoons which in parts was suitable for settlement but which was probably more extensively used as a hunting ground. The first East Anglian Mesolithic settlers seem to have crossed the land bridge from Denmark and the Baltic about 7000 B.C. bringing with them the *Maglemosian* culture. This move westwards was not a definite migration but rather a drift of men moving to new hunting grounds.

Our knowledge of these people in East Anglia comes from a limited number of sites which have produced no remains of habitation other than assemblages of flint implements and waste flakes.

Continental excavations have shown that the Maglemosian hunter-fishers lived beside the edges of lakes, on the banks of rivers and along the coast, and that their economy was largely based on the catching of whatever fish, animals and birds could be found within the immediate environment and East Anglian evidence agrees well with this.

At Kelling near the north Norfolk coast the Maglemosians occupied a site on the heath-covered upper slopes of a gravel plateau which rises to about 200 feet above sea level; their occupation is shown by the number of flint implements which have been found there. These had been made on the spot using flint from the gravel plateau itself. The main types of tools were points, varying from one to two inches in length and with one edge blunted; horseshoe-shaped scrapers; irregularly shaped flint flakes; and a form of axe or pick often quite roughly finished off (fig. 6). This assemblage bears very close relationships to material from the European Maglemosian sites from which it very obviously derives, and also is very similar to that from another East Anglian site, Two Mile Bottom near Thetford. Here, near the right bank of the Little Ouse, another occupation site has produced flint implements conforming to those at Kelling; these two places probably represent temporary encampments of Mesolithic man who changed his habitation seasonally in response to the movement of game.

Other sites in East Anglia can be found beside lakes and along the river valleys. At Spong Heath, on the edge of Hockham Mere, an arrowhead and some microlithic points with distinct affinities to the Two Mile Bottom series give evidence of Mesolithic settlement. In the valley of the Wensum the sites of Hellesdon, Sparham and Lyng have produced flints in some quantity, although in some cases the association of apparently Mesolithic types with later flint forms makes dating difficult. It may be that on some sites Mesolithic traditions existed side by side with much later Neolithic and even Bronze Age traditions and this suggests that Mesolithic traits continued beyond the end of the period.

Although most of the evidence that we have for Maglemosian man in East Anglia comes from collections of flint implements, we know from other areas, where the preservation conditions are more favourable, that one of the dominant characteristics of Mesolithic culture was the use made of bone. Unfortunately, no sites have so far been discovered in East Anglia where the conditions have been right for the preservation of organic material and we have to rely on other sites to give us some idea of the true wealth and variety of the material objects of Maglemosian man. The site of Star Carr in Yorkshire, excavated by Professor Grahame Clark in 1949–51, has shown that an enormous amount of organic material can be discovered on a waterlogged site. This site is of a somewhat earlier date than those in East Anglia, being occupied from about 8000 to 7000 B.C., but it seems fair to assume that the East Anglian Maglemosian culture made use of similar objects. There is in East Anglia, however, one object of bone belonging to this period which has been preserved in a remarkable manner. In 1931 a fishing boat, trawling in the North Sea near the Leman and Ower Banks northeast of Cromer, dredged up a complete

bone harpoon (fig. 6). This is very similar to types found in Estonia and was no doubt used, attached to a wooden shaft, as a fish harpoon. The diagonal scratches at the lower end of the implement are an aid to a more firm hafting. This object with its very high quality workmanship can give us some idea of the amount of fine material we must have lost, and it also provides interesting evidence for the occupation of at least

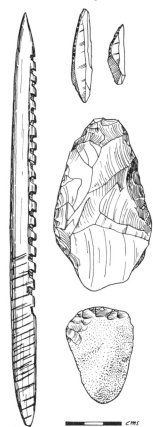

Fig. 6 *Implements of the Maglemosian culture: bone harpoon from the North Sea (left); flint points (above), axe (centre), and end scraper from Kelling*

22

the more southerly part of what is now the North Sea at the period around 7000 B.C.

The evidence for Maglemosian occupation of East Anglia has come almost exclusively from surface finds and unstratified sites, and therefore our knowledge can only be incomplete and unsatisfactory.

THE SAUVETERRIANS: PEACOCK'S FARM

Fortunately, in the next phase of the Mesolithic period, the *Sauveterrian*, there is at least one well-stratified excavated site, Peacock's Farm, Shippea Hill (fig. 7). This lies, in fact, in Cambridgeshire, strictly just outside our area, but its position on the edge of the fens and its obvious association with a site in

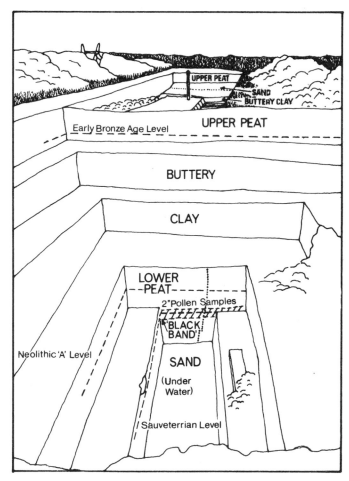

UPPER PEAT

SAND

BUTTERY CLAY

Early Bronze Age Level

UPPER PEAT

BUTTERY

CLAY

LOWER PEAT

2" Pollen Samples

'BLACK BAND'

Neolithic 'A' Level

SAND

(Under Water)

Sauveterrian Level

Fig. 7 *Excavations at Peacock's Farm: section*

23

north-west Suffolk—Wangford near Lakenheath—justify its inclusion. Excavations at Peacock's Farm revealed a sequence of Mesolithic, Neolithic and Bronze Age layers in peat beds, all in land lying below present sea level. Flints from the lowest layer: narrow flakes, flint cores bearing scars of narrow flakes, microliths and microburins (fig. 8), show that they belong to the

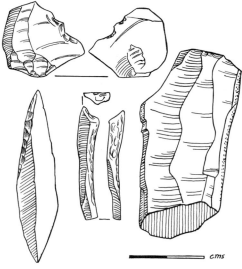

Fig. 8 *Microliths from Peacock's Farm*

Sauveterrian culture. Samples from within the Mesolithic layer have given a radiocarbon date of 5650 ± 150 years B.C., and from the top of the layer a date of 4735 ± 150 years B.C. It therefore seems that the Mesolithic occupation of Peacock's Farm lasted for almost one thousand years, spanning the latter part

of the sixth and the early part of the fifth millennia B.C. Analysis of pollen grains within the Mesolithic layer gives an outline of the vegetation of the area at the period of occupation; basically, the countryside contained woodland trees, mainly pine but with frequent elm, oak and hazel. There was also some more open heathland with bracken and grass.

The Sauveterrian people preferred to live on sandy, open heaths, in generally treeless regions. Their possible area of occupation in East Anglia was limited, therefore, to the edge of the fens; as, for example, at both Peacock's Farm and at Wangford. Since their habitat was treeless they did not make implements for timber working; this contrasts strongly with the tools of the Maglemosian culture.

The people of both cultures, however, were very similar in their economy and general way of life, although the Maglemosians came originally from the Baltic region and the Sauveterrians were either descendants of indigenous Upper Palaeolithic hunters or arrived in Britain from France or Belgium at some time before the final broaching of the English Channel, about 5000 B.C. Once established, both groups appear to have existed side by side in East Anglia, each restricted to its own environment—by the water in the case of the Maglemosians and in open country for the Sauveterrians. The climate of the later part of the Mesolithic period—from 5000 B.C. onwards—was warm and moist; this encouraged the expansion of deciduous forest which increased the isolation of the East Anglian population.

4 The First Farmers: The Neolithic

In the fourth millennium (c. 3400) B.C. further groups of immigrants arrived on the shores of the British Isles from continental Europe. These new arrivals of the *Neolithic* culture settled extensively throughout the lowland areas of Britain, gradually overcame or absorbed the native Mesolithic population, and were responsible for introducing agriculture into the British Isles.

This basic change, from hunting, fishing and food-gathering to the domestication of animals and the raising of crops, marks the break between the Mesolithic and Neolithic periods; it is often called the 'Neolithic Revolution'. The implications of such a revolution are enormous; once an organized agricultural economy is adopted, permanent settlements must be formed and the archaeologist may now hope to find not only tools, but the remains of settlements themselves. The introduction of permanent settlements also led to the use of collective burial sites, and the methods employed in burying the dead can give us information about the more intangible aspects of prehistoric society, such as religious belief and ritual.

At this point we also find for the first time one of the most valuable aids for understanding the past—pottery. This has so far been missing from our list of possible sources of information, but from now onwards it will play an ever-increasing role in the interpretation of prehistory. As in the Mesolithic period,

organic materials such as wood or bone have not generally been preserved in the ground, but fired clay is a material which is virtually indestructible and from the Neolithic period onwards it is the most frequently found man-made object. Pottery is used in the later periods very much in the same way as flints are used in earlier periods in the interpretation of man's development.

Neolithic man arrived in Britain from Europe during the early or middle part of the fourth millennium B.C., bringing with him his own tradition of crop raising, animal breeding, pottery making and stone working. Domestication of animals had been known in the Middle East from much earlier times; there is, for instance, evidence for domesticated sheep in Iran about 9000 B.C., and for pigs and cattle shortly afterwards. Similarly, the cultivation of cereals thrived in the East and when the first Neolithic settlers of Britain arrived they brought with them barley, einkorn and emmer, all of eastern origin. On their arrival in Britain they found themselves in a countryside dominated by mixed oak forest and an environment which had only slightly been affected by the activities of the Mesolithic hunters. At Peacock's Farm, for example, pollen analysis of the Mesolithic peat deposits indicated only very slight changes in the dominant vegetation despite the long period of human occupation on the site.

One of the most spectacular results of

the arrival of Neolithic man in the British Isles is the sharp decrease in the proportion of elm to other tree species; this has been shown at a number of sites where Neolithic peat deposits have been investigated. It was originally thought that the decline of elm was caused by climatic changes, but more recently it has been suggested that the introduction of domestic animals by Neolithic man necessitated the extensive collection of leaf fodder, and elm appears to have been the species to suffer most.

Neolithic man also influenced his environment by raising crops. At the beginning of the period a moderate amount of forest clearance was carried out to provide land for crop raising, and this is recorded in pollen analyses by the appearance of weed species associated with agriculture.

Our knowledge of the Neolithic period owes a great deal to scientific aids which have been applied to archaeological problems over the past decade or so. The most valuable of these is that known as the radiocarbon or C^{14} method of dating organic material. More and more samples are now being dated by this method and the result is that there are now a number of precise dates for significant Neolithic sites, to which more are being added yearly. In 1954 it was suggested that the British Neolithic period occupied roughly 500 years from about 2000 B.C. C^{14} dating has shown that this estimate must be radically changed and it is now generally accepted that the Neolithic began in Britain about 3400 B.C. and lasted well into the second millennium B.C. The period therefore covered a time span of almost 2000 years, and within this lengthy period there are a number of subdivisions.

The Neolithic period in the British Isles is basically divided into Early, Middle and Late phases, all of which are represented on East Anglian sites.

PEACOCK'S FARM: THE NEOLITHIC SETTLEMENT

The earliest Neolithic site in East Anglia is that at Peacock's Farm, Shippea Hill, which has already been mentioned as an important site of the Mesolithic period. Habitation on the site was by no means continuous from the Mesolithic to the Neolithic; radiocarbon dating of the two phases suggests a gap of well over a thousand years between the two stages of occupation.

Excavations revealed no structures, but there was an occupation layer containing sheep bones and sherds of plain, well-made, round-bottomed pots (fig. 9) which are characteristic of the earliest pottery made in this country. Traditions of pottery making were brought to the British Isles by settlers from the Continent, and the earliest Neolithic pottery of this type (conventionally known as Windmill Hill pottery from the site in Wiltshire where it was first identified) is found throughout southern and eastern Britain. It is therefore assumed that the earliest farmers first settled in these more southerly regions, probably on the land which was most easily cleared and cultivated. From this viewpoint Peacock's Farm was well suited to early settlement because of its position between the marshy fenland which provided water, and the more open and less wooded area of the breckland with its light, sandy soil. Unfortunately, this site gives little material information about the houses and way of life of the settlers, but it is of prime archaeological impor-

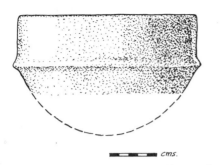

Fig. 9 *Bowl of the Windmill Hill type from Peacock's Farm*

tance in that the peat layer in which the Neolithic material was found has produced startling results both from C^{14} dating and from pollen analyses. A large number of samples were taken for radiocarbon dating and an average date for the earliest Neolithic occupation on the site has been estimated at 3400 B.C. This is now taken as a probable date for the beginning of the Neolithic in the British Isles as a whole. Pollen samples showed a decline of elm associated with the increase of bracken and other plants of the open country.

From both the archaeological material and the scientific evidence we can build up a picture of the life of the Neolithic settlers at Peacock's Farm. In about 3400 B.C. they arrived at a wooded area on the margin of the fenland and the breckland, bringing with them a tradition of pottery making, crop raising and animal husbandry. They then proceeded to clear at least a small part of the surrounding woodland for agricultural purposes and conducted a subsistence economy. This form of settlement and occupation appears to have been typical of the early Neolithic settlement of the British Isles.

THE MIDDLE NEOLITHIC PERIOD

During the first half of the third millennium B.C. the Early Neolithic gave way to the *Middle Neolithic*. This latter period lasted from about 2850 to about 2000 B.C. and there are a number of characteristics which distinguish it from the preceding period. By no means all of these characteristic features are found in East Anglia, but the area appears to have had a flourishing economy and an increased number of inhabitants at this time. Once again the economic emphasis was on animal husbandry and crop raising, and East Anglian settlement was mainly in the two light-soil centres of the breckland and the Ipswich region. The heavily wooded Boulder Clay area of High Norfolk and High Suffolk was still uninhabited and served to isolate the two centres of population.

The Middle Neolithic reached the peak of its development in Wessex—Hampshire and Wiltshire—and cultural influences spread outwards from there to the rest of England. East Anglia's link with the Wessex region was tenuous and entirely confined to the route along the chalk ridge—the Icknield Way. In contrast to its important position in the early Neolithic, East Anglia now appears to be only marginal to Neolithic cultural development and there are many features of the fully developed Wessex Middle Neolithic which are absent from the region.

Although agriculture was still the mainstay of the Neolithic economy, a flourishing trade seems to have been developing in the export of stone axes from their centres of production in the west to the rest of the British Isles. Axes were essential equipment for Neolithic man, who was attempting to extend his area of settlement by forest clearance, and there were relatively few areas of Britain where suitable fine-grained stone could easily be found. The expansion of this trade appears to be bound up with the *causewayed camps* of central and south-west England which, originally thought to have been cattle corrals, are now interpreted as centres of seasonal gatherings of people for both the interchange of goods (fairs) and religious observances. Such camps, characteristic features of the Neolithic period, are missing from the East Anglian scene, although contact with the Wessex area is suggested by the discovery at Hurst Fen, Mildenhall, of a polished stone axe which comes from the Lake District but has also been found in the causewayed camps.

HURST FEN

Other aspects of the Middle Neolithic, however, are represented in the East Anglian material. As in the earlier period, knowledge of house types is very limited, and from East Anglia there are no well-attested remains of Neolithic buildings, but there are a number of sites which provide evidence for occupation. One of these is at Hurst Fen, which, like Peacock's Farm, lies between the breckland and the fenland, about one and a half miles north of the River Lark and some miles to the west of the Icknield Way. It gives further evidence for the importance of occupation near the fens during the Neolithic period— the fens serving not only as a source of water, but also as a suitable hunting ground for birds and fish.

The settlement at Hurst Fen represents only one of a number of Middle Neolithic sites which cluster around the south-east corner of the fens on the borders of present-day Suffolk and Cambridgeshire. All these sites are distinguished by the presence of a type of pottery known as *Mildenhall ware,* and a laurel-leaf shaped flint point of a projectile (fig. 10). The Mildenhall pottery represents a regional variation of the basic Windmill Hill pottery which was present at Peacock's Farm in the early period and which persisted in Wessex throughout the Middle Neolithic; the flints, similarly, are a purely East Anglian development. Fig. 11 shows the distribution of these two features, but it is only at Hurst Fen itself that excavation has produced more material evidence for the life of the inhabitants.

No house remains have been revealed with certainty, but the presence of a number of pits suggests that the site was occupied permanently; these pits, often lined with wattle, were used for storage or as cellars, mainly for grain. They have been found not only in western East Anglia, but also over much of lowland England where arable farming was the basis of the economy. Each cluster of pits may represent the wealth of one family and therefore one dwelling, but the actual house remains at Hurst Fen have disappeared and it is impossible to say what sort of houses were occupied or indeed how many families lived there at any one time.

The inhabitants lived by cultivating emmer and barley and by keeping cattle, pigs, sheep and goats. They supplemented their diet by hunting, using flint arrowheads and javelins to catch their prey. Some forest clearance took place with the aid of polished greenstone axes from the Lake District, and the women of the community made the dis-

28

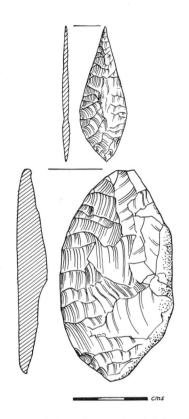

Fig. 10 *Leaf-shaped arrowhead (above) and laurel-leaf flint from Hurst Fen*

this is one of the first examples of contact between the two main centres of East Anglian population through the main east–west valley route. There seems also to have been a string of settlements south-westwards down the Icknield Way. In the Chilterns Mildenhall pottery is found together with local wares and indicates that there were trading contacts between East Anglia and the rest of Britain at this time.

BURIAL CUSTOMS: COLLECTIVE GRAVES

East Anglia is sharply distinguished from other parts of the British Isles in that the method of burial used in the region in the Middle Neolithic period is almost unknown. The usual method in the rest of the country was the interment under long mounds of disarticulated bodies which had previously been exposed in a mortuary chamber. Such long earth mounds or *barrows* occur extensively in much of lowland England while in highland areas they are replaced by large stone tombs or megaliths. East Anglia is remarkably poor in such remains and only four Neolithic barrows are known from the region. Three of these are in Norfolk: two on West Rudham Common and one on Broome Heath, Ditchingham. The remaining one, Swales Tumulus at Worlington in Suffolk, produced an unusual combination of Neolithic and Bronze Age burial, the earlier possibly having some associations with the Hurst Fen people.

tinctive Mildenhall pottery with its soft corky texture, the clay sometimes mixed with crushed flints and sand. One of the most clearly marked differences between it and the earlier Windmill Hill type was that now much of the pottery was decorated with incised lines and stab marks. Pottery may have been quite precious as some of the pots from Hurst Fen appear to have been repaired.

Mildenhall ware is found not only in the fenland (fig. 11), but also along the Gipping valley and in the coastal lowlands of south Suffolk and north Essex;

Swales Tumulus consists of a small Neolithic mound covered by a later and larger Bronze Age barrow. A body appears to have been cremated on a funeral pyre and subsequently covered by a simple earth mound. The pottery associated with the burial shows some Hurst

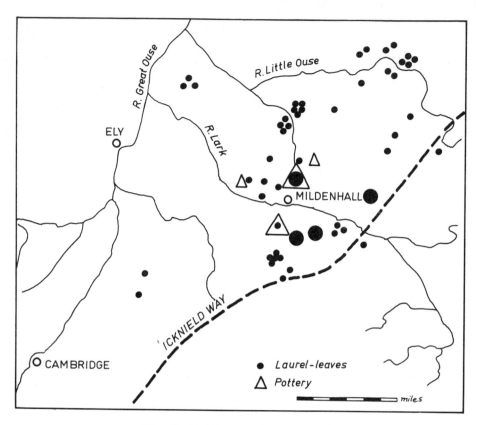

Fig. 11 *Distribution of Hurst Fen elements*

Fen affinities, but there are also some sherds of the finer pot of the Windmill Hill type and it may be that Swales Tumulus contains a burial belonging either to the Early Neolithic period, or to a people whose culture was a combination of earlier and later traits.

Of the remaining burials, one at West Rudham has been excavated. This shows that the mound covered a platform cremation. The body was first placed on an open wooden platform and cremated; the remains were then covered by a mound of turf sods, and finally the whole surmounted by a layer of earth which was dug from a ditch around the barrow. The final size of the mound appears to have been about 240 feet × 70 feet. This type of platform cremation under a mound is known from Wessex but rarely occurs elsewhere. The method of construction with turf sods can be paralleled by the nearest barrow to West Rudham, 60 miles to the south-west at Therfield Heath, Royston, but otherwise the barrow type is most unusual and may represent a degenerate form, lying as it does far from the centre of the Middle

Neolithic culture in Wessex. It may, on the other hand, belong to a very late phase of the Neolithic period, but our knowledge of Neolithic burial customs in East Anglia is so slight that it is impossible to put forward any definite theories on the basis of the West Rudham excavation.

LATE NEOLITHIC: PETERBOROUGH WARE

The last phase of the Neolithic period in East Anglia is mainly distinguishable by the types of pottery in use. The two main pottery types are known as Peterborough ware and Rinyo-Clacton ware, both of them deriving from the earlier Neolithic traditions of the Windmill Hill ware, but at the same time influenced by native Mesolithic traits which persisted throughout the earlier phases of the Neolithic. In East Anglia we have most information about the makers of *Peterborough ware,* a heavy, coarse, round-bottomed type of pottery with a thickened rim and whipped cord decoration (fig. 12). Sites producing this pottery are found mainly in the breckland, which once again proves to be the most densely populated East Anglian district. But there must also have been occupation in the north-east of the region for, at Arminghall, near Norwich, excavation has shown the existence of a *henge monument* connected with the religious beliefs and practices of the Peterborough people.

NEOLITHIC RELIGION: HENGE MONUMENTS

A henge consists of a roughly circular enclosure, surrounded by a bank and ditch broken by either one or two entrances. The Arminghall henge has a single entrance and a central area 90 feet

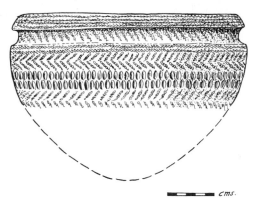

Fig. 12 *Bowl of Peterborough ware*

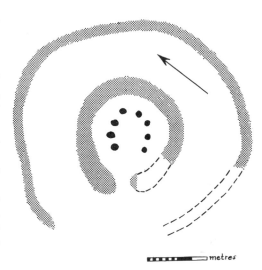

Fig. 13 *Plan of Arminghall henge monument*

in diameter enclosed by an inner and outer ditch and an intervening earth bank (fig. 13). Within the central space eight large holes, each about $7\frac{1}{2}$ feet deep and 3 feet in diameter, were arranged in a horseshoe shape with its open end opposite the main entrance. These had originally supported large timber posts. Such henge monuments are well known, particularly in central southern England

—Stonehenge itself gave its name to these monuments—and most of them seem to be associated with running water. This is true both of Arminghall and of an unexcavated example in Suffolk at Stratford St. Mary on the north bank of the River Stour.

Arminghall henge was built, by people of the Peterborough ware tradition, *c.* 2500 B.C. and it continued as a religious centre throughout the remaining years of the third millenniun. It was finally taken over and developed by the next group of immigrants, the Beaker people, who arrived in Britain around the year 2000 B.C.

FLINT MINES

Another activity associated with the Peterborough people is the mining of flint. Until the end of the Middle Neolithic period all flint used in tool-making came from surface finds. About the end of the third millennium, however, demand for high-quality flint increased and this encouraged suitable areas to develop a mining industry. Foremost among these was East Anglia where the Upper Chalk, covering so much of High Norfolk and High Suffolk, contains beds of very fine quality flint which is relatively easy to extract.

Several groups of mines have been discovered in East Anglia: Grimes Graves and Lynford in the breckland; Great Massingham near the prehistoric trackway of Peddars Way in north-west Norfolk; and Whitlingham, Buckenham Tofts and Ringland in the Norwich region. Of these, the mines at Grimes Graves are the best known and have been the most thoroughly investigated. Radiocarbon dates indicate that the mines were being worked from about

2400 B.C. to 1600 B.C., with the busiest period around 2000 B.C.

The flint was obtained either through open-cast mining or by a much more elaborate method of sinking shafts and linking them together by horizontal galleries. There are surface indications of over three hundred pits and shafts at Grimes Graves, but only a limited number were in use at any one time. The miners used picks made of red deer antler, crowbars of long-bones, and wedges of flint for prising out the raw material. They worked underground by the light of simple lamps made of hollowed-out lumps of chalk in which a wick floated in oil or grease. They conducted religious ceremonies to ensure the productivity of the mines, and a group of seven antler picks, a lamp and some crudely carved chalk objects were found as a dedication deposit in one of the pits.

Once the flint had been produced from the mine-shafts it was roughly trimmed to shape on the nearby working floors where one can find both waste flint flakes from the roughing-out process and some partly finished axes. They were then distributed in the surrounding countryside where they would be finished to the desired shape by the customer himself. Once metal became common for tool-making the East Anglian flint mines were no longer necessary and they were abandoned by the middle of the second millennium B.C.

Little can be said about the settlements of the Peterborough people. Their economy, based on stock breeding and trade, rather than arable farming, may not have encouraged the development of permanent settlements and the slight traces that remain may be from temporary seasonal camps. This rather unsettled way of life may be inherited from the indigenous Mesolithic population whose traditions are represented in Peterborough pottery.

RINYO–CLACTON PEOPLE

The second group of Late Neolithic people in East Anglia are those who made the *Rinyo-Clacton* type of pottery, sometimes called *Grooved ware*. The most common form of pot was a flat-bottomed bowl elaborately decorated with incised triangles and lozenges (fig. 14). The people associated with this type of pottery lived in all parts of the British Isles, but, while the northern areas show remains of a rich culture, sites in East Anglia are comparatively poor.

The main centres of population are once again the breckland and Ipswich regions, with outliers on the north-east Norfolk coast. One of the most important Rinyo-Clacton sites is at Honington in breckland Suffolk. The inhabitants of this settlement appear to have lived in huts or tents of very flimsy construction and to have done their cooking in the open air. Their flint tools suggest that they hunted game with bow and arrow, practised some form of carpentry and cut local rushes for thatch or basket making. The discovery of grain storage pits nearby suggests that the Rinyo-Clacton folk gained at least part of their livelihood from arable farming. Another Suffolk site, Creeting St. Mary near Ipswich, has produced storage pits associated with Rinyo-Clacton pottery, but, as with the Peterborough people, arable farming probably did not play a greater part in their economy than stock raising and hunting. Both sites are in low-lying ground close to water, Creeting

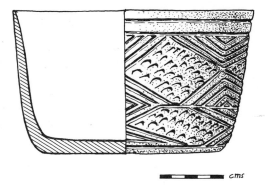

Fig. 14 *Bowl of Rinyo-Clacton ware from Creeting St. Mary*

St. Mary near a tributary of the River Gipping and Honington on the Black Bourn which runs into the Little Ouse. This seems typical of Rinyo-Clacton settlements in south-eastern England and may indicate some economic dependence on fishing.

THE BEAKER PEOPLE

Both the Peterborough and Rinyo-Clacton people lived side by side in East Anglia throughout the Late Neolithic, but their numbers were supplemented about 2000 B.C. by immigrants who arrived in Britain from the Low Countries. These new arrivals brought with them a type of pottery which is characteristic of their culture and which gives them their name—the *Beaker people*. The vessels, popularly supposed to have been used for beer drinking, are divided into three classes: the Longnecked or A-Beaker, the Bell or B-Beaker and the Shortnecked or C-Beaker. All three types are remarkable for their very high quality and elaborate decoration which consists of numerous geometric designs either impressed or incised into the clay, and these designs influenced the East

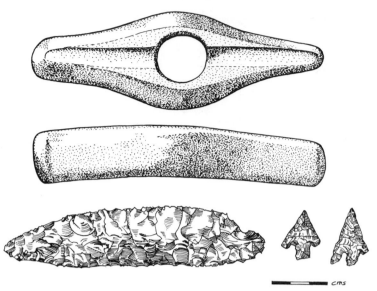

cms

Fig. 15 *Early Bronze Age implements and weapons: stone battle-axe (above) from Toft Monks; flint sickle from Mildenhall; barbed-and-tanged arrowheads from Plantation Farm*

Anglian pottery makers so much that a hybrid type of pottery, *Rusticated ware*, developed which incorporated both indigenous traits and new ideas.

The Beaker people were the first in Britain to use metal tools, but they did not work bronze themselves and their simple tools all seem to have been imported from elsewhere. No metal objects have been found in Beaker contexts in East Anglia and all their equipment is of flint or stone in the true Neolithic tradition, although some of the shapes suggest that the flint knappers were copying metal objects. Barbed-and-tanged arrowheads (fig. 15) which replace the laurel-leaf arrowheads of the earlier Neolithic, polished stone battle-axes (fig. 15) and polished-edge flint knives all imitate metal prototypes. The implements associated with the Beaker culture, including such things as bone wrist

guards for bowmen, seem primarily to be warlike in character, but more peaceful pursuits are indicated by a flint sickle blade (fig. 15) from Mildenhall.

Arable farming seems to have played some part in the Beaker economy and grain storage pits have been found on sites at Edingthorpe in Norfolk, Lakenheath in Suffolk and Hayland House at Mildenhall. At Edingthorpe, clusters of pits were found associated with so-called hut floors, and other occupation sites, notably those on the fen edges, have produced bones both of domesticated animals—ox, sheep or goat and pig—as well as red deer and roe deer. One can assume that the economy of the Beaker people was basically one of mixed farming supplemented by hunting, but the scarcity of Beaker settlement sites makes it impossible to be more specific.

One of the main features which distinguishes the Beaker people from the earlier Neolithic peoples is their method of burial which changed from mass burials under long barrows, to individual interment, sometimes beneath a small low, round mound, sometimes in a flat grave. The bodies were buried in a crouched position, either with or without grave goods; but in East Anglia we have very few skeletal remains because bones have often been destroyed through the acidity of the soil, and our knowledge of Beaker burials is as slight as that of their settlements.

5 Metal-using Peoples: The Bronze Age

Metal technology, the smelting of ore and the forging of tools and weapons, originated, like agriculture, in the Middle East. The earliest metal objects of all were made of pure copper, but this is a soft metal and cannot take a cutting edge; it was found that an alloy consisting of nine parts copper to one part tin was harder than pure copper and more suitable for tool-making. This alloy is known as bronze. The knowledge of bronze did not reach the British Isles until very much later and it seems probable that our first native bronzes were made in Ireland where the presence of copper ores made technical developments practicable.

The *Bronze Age* in Britain lasted for rather more than 1100 years from about 1650 B.C. and our knowledge of the period is very patchy. Many blanks remain to be filled in, notably about settlements and dwellings, but on the other hand some aspects of the Bronze Age have been very well explored and we know a great deal about the material possessions of the people, particularly in the later phases of the period.

Unlike agriculture, which was introduced by immigrant peoples, the Bronze Age in the British Isles developed through the native populations adapting their cultures to new technological advances, and bronze did not immediately supersede all the flint implements of the Neolithic period. At first the new material was scarce and expensive and therefore confined to the wealthier members of society; the spread of bronze tools was slow, especially in the Early Bronze Age when all implements were imported from Ireland, and it was not until the Middle or Late Bronze Age that bronzes became more common and were produced in local workshops. Once this happened the use of bronze tools and weapons became more widespread, but even so, flint implements never went completely out of use and in East Anglia they were being made throughout the whole of the Bronze Age and even into the Iron Age.

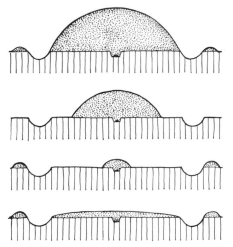

Fig. 16 *Types of round barrow: bowl, bell, disc and saucer barrows*

THE WESSEX CULTURE IN EAST ANGLIA: AN INTRUSIVE ELEMENT

The part of Britain which first adopted a fully developed Bronze Age culture was Wessex, whose people, acting as middlemen in the Irish bronze trade, accumulated great wealth which they displayed in their lavish burials and magnificent monuments, such as Stonehenge. Our knowledge of the *Wessex* culture comes mainly from burial customs which consisted of inhumation under a barrow (fig. 16), accompanied by very rich grave goods, often gold, amber or faience (blue glass) ornaments and imported bronze weapons. Once the initial impetus of the bronze trade had worn off, the wealth of the Wessex culture declined and in its second phase, 1500 to 1400 B.C., there are signs of general degeneration; inhumation gives way to cremation, grave goods are very much poorer and there is little indication of contact with the outside world. The main influence of the Wessex culture in East Anglia can be

seen in a group of burials in the west of the region, where a number of barrows containing rich grave goods are clustered close to the Icknield Way.

The barrow at Little Cressingham, Norfolk, contained goods of an early Wessex character; a bell barrow covered a male inhumation whose grave goods included two bronze daggers, amber beads and decorative plaques of sheet gold. Other objects representative of the Wessex culture have been found in East Anglia; for instance, gold-covered beads from South Barrow, Great Bircham, a bronze dagger from a barrow at Chippenham near Newmarket and blue faience segmented beads. It has been suggested that the Wessex burials in East Anglia represent a small ruling minority who gained sway over the East Anglian natives through their greater wealth; they left few other remains, but the material that they introduced into East Anglia was important in influencing the native Bronze Age cultures there.

THE EAST ANGLIAN EARLY BRONZE AGE: THE FOOD VESSEL CULTURE

The Early Bronze Age in East Anglia is mainly represented by a population which belonged to the *Food Vessel* culture and who occupied much of Norfolk and Suffolk from about 1650 to 1400 B.C. The characteristic pottery which gives them their name consists of a coarsely made jar of poorly fired clay, usually highly decorated with finger-nail impressions (fig. 17). Both the shape and decoration indicate that the pottery is descended from Peterborough and Beaker prototypes and is closely related to wares from Yorkshire where the Food Vessel culture is concentrated.

Most of our knowledge of the people

Fig. 17 *Collared Urn (left) from Icklingham and Food Vessel from Mildenhall*

of the Food Vessel culture comes from their graves; both crouched inhumation and cremation were practised and frequently the burials were concealed beneath a barrow. Food vessels were often placed with the dead, as at Warren Hill, Mildenhall, and Pakenham, Grimstone End, both in Suffolk, but a distinctive type of pottery was developed to accompany or contain cremated remains. These, known as *Collared Urns* (fig. 17), are found fairly frequently in Suffolk where they represent the most usual form of Bronze Age burial. They are descended from Peterborough ware and bear some very distinctive features of the earlier tradition as, for instance, the whipped cord type of decoration on both the inner and outer faces of the vessels. The urns either contained cremated remains, or were placed upside-down over the ashes and then were covered by a small bell barrow. These barrows are either isolated or, more frequently, form groups of half a dozen or so which

may be cemeteries belonging to a family or clan.

SETTLEMENTS ON THE FEN EDGES: PLANTATION FARM

Very few Early Bronze Age settlement sites have been discovered or excavated, and it may be that the Food Vessel people were pastoralists living in temporary encampments. Some sites on the fen edges have, however, produced occupation material of Early Bronze Age character. From one of these, Plantation Farm, Shippea Hill, we know that the population lived on a sandy ridge surrounded by alder swamps which provided them with fishing grounds. Nearby lay the higher breckland where cattle, sheep, goats and pigs were grazed and red deer were hunted with barbed-and-tanged arrows. Stock breeding seems to have been their main occupation although some notched and serrated tools from the site may have been used as sickles for harvesting crops. Flint scrapers for the preparation of hides, plano-convex knives and awls made up the rest of their equipment. Similar tools have been found at Peacock's Farm nearby and also a little further away at Joist Fen, New Fen and Right-Up Drove, all near Lakenheath. Occupation at Plantation Farm appears to have come to an end when the climate became damper and made the sand ridge no longer suitable for habitation. Perhaps the population then moved away to higher ground on the fen edge, to sites such as those near Lakenheath.

The material from all these sites is completely lacking in bronze objects and the Food Vessel people obviously practised an extensive flint industry within a nominally Bronze Age culture. It is not until the later phases of the Bronze Age that the East Anglian people began to use bronze tools and weapons in any quantity; this happened when itinerant bronze smiths began to carry with them collections of scrap metal for melting down and working into new implements. Even in the bronze-rich later periods bronzes are seldom found in connection with settlement debris, they are most frequently found in hoards. The number of hoards from the Early Bronze Age is, however, very small, so that our knowledge of Early Bronze Age metal equipment is scanty even from this source. Four flanged axes were found at Holywell Row, Mildenhall, and a larger collection of twenty-one flanged axes and some gold rings have been found at Hall Farm, Postlingford, Suffolk.

THE MIDDLE BRONZE AGE

During much of the *Middle Bronze Age* there was little contact between East Anglia and other parts of Britain, and Food Vessels and Collared Urns continued

Fig. 18 *Bronze Age pottery: Biconical Urn from Hollesley*

in use together with *Biconical Urns* (fig. 18) which were developed from them. Late in the period external influences can be seen in the emergence of *Barrel and Bucket Urns*.

Nearly all the pottery comes from burials which are simple urned cremations. The first phase of the Middle Bronze Age is characterized by the continuation of burial within barrows, either as secondary burials within an already existing mound, or in totally new structures. Cremation urns have been found in barrows at Icklingham and Chillesford, both in Suffolk, but at Risby, Suffolk, a barrow burial contained a cremation without an urn.

URNFIELDS AND THE DEVEREL-RIMBURY PEOPLE

About 1200 B.C. the *Deverel-Rimbury people* arrived in southern Britain from north France and the Low Countries and brought with them both a new economy, which included the use of the plough, and new burial customs. These people made their greatest impact on the population of Wessex and Sussex, but cultural influences penetrated to the more distant parts of the country, including East Anglia. Their influence here is most strongly shown by the introduction of the Bucket Urn to contain cremations which are buried not in barrows but in flat urnfields. But in some parts of the region local developments were taking place with no regard for the rest of the country as, for instance, in south-east Suffolk where a type of cremation urn evolved through the fusion of Neolithic Rinyo-Clacton ware, Rusticated ware and Necked Beakers. South-east Suffolk seems to have been cut off from the more westerly regions by the wooded Boulder Clay lands and was more open to seaward influences than to any from inland. The types of pottery developed here and elsewhere in East Anglia during the Middle Bronze Age continued with little change throughout the succeeding period.

MIDDLE AND LATE BRONZE AGE SETTLEMENTS: MILDENHALL

Two sites in Suffolk, lying in the area between the fenland and the breckland, give the best evidence for the settlements of the Middle and Late Bronze Age people. Neither has produced any traces of house types, but excavations have given us a good idea of the economy of the inhabitants.

Both sites, Mildenhall Fen and Wilde Street, Mildenhall, lie on high ground at the edge of the fens; throughout the Middle and Late Bronze Ages a damper climate caused the fens to become progressively more waterlogged and occupation moved away from the fen proper to

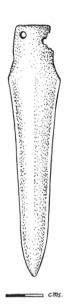

cms.

Fig. 19 *Bronze knife from Wilde Street, Mildenhall*

the drier ground on the edge. The site at Mildenhall Fen was, in fact, covered by peat shortly after its abandonment during the Late Bronze Age, as a result of the damp conditions.

The settlements were the bases for mixed farmers who concentrated rather more on stock breeding than crop raising. Domestic animals included pig, sheep or goat, and cattle, with dogs used for rounding them up. Hunting played a considerable part in increasing the food supply, and red deer, roe deer, otter and wildfowl were the most common prey. A flint quern, or grinding stone, at Mildenhall Fen shows that some cereals were grown. As in the Early Bronze Age, most tools used on the sites were made of flint, although at Wilde Street a simple bronze knife was found and this is the only example from the whole of East Anglia of a bronze implement actually found on an occupation site (fig. 19). The population used the same types of flint tools as in the earlier period of the Bronze Age except that the barbed-and-tanged arrowheads are missing; but the general standard of flint working is very low and more force than skill seems to have been used.

Bone working was also an important part of life on the sites, and awls, needles and pins were found in some numbers. Bone knife handles were also made and one may have been used for the hafting of the bronze knife at Wilde Street.

Pottery on both sites was coarse and ill-fired and follows the main character-

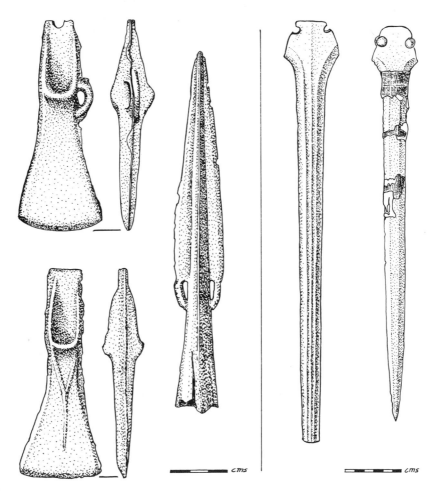

Fig. 20 *Middle Bronze Age weapons: palstaves (axes) and spearhead from the Stibbard hoard; rapiers from Thetford (left) and West Row*

istics of the Deverel-Rimbury types, although it also exhibits native traits of the Late Neolithic and Early Bronze Age. The Mildenhall sites may represent the settlements of peoples of Deverel-Rimbury traditions who merged with an already established population. Certainly, the economy of the sites seems little different from that practised by the Early Bronze Age peoples although there may have been a greater emphasis on crop raising.

BRONZE HOARDS

Although we know very little of Middle Bronze Age metal objects from settlements, we have a considerable amount of information on the development of East Anglian bronze working in this period. Our knowledge comes from the discovery of groups of bronze implements or hoards, either founders' hoards—scrap collected together by a smith for melting down and reworking—or personal hoards consisting of only two or three objects which had either been lost or deliberately deposited, perhaps as a religious observance.

One of the most extensive hoards from the Middle Bronze Age in East Anglia is that from Stibbard, Norfolk, which contained socketed spearheads with basal loops and palstaves (axes) both with and without loops (fig. 20). Both these types were intended to be hafted on a wooden shaft, using the loops to increase the firmness with which the metal could be attached to the wood. Spearheads and palstaves are typical Middle Bronze Age weapons and, together with the rapier, formed the armoury of a Middle Bronze Age warrior. Many rapiers are known from East Anglia, particularly from the fenland, some made there, others im-

ported. During the middle phase of the Middle Bronze Age, about the twelfth or eleventh century B.C., a local bronze-working industry grew up in western East Anglia at first specializing in the so-called Thetford class of rapier which was designed for thrusting rather than slashing. Other forms were also developed, notably a slashing rapier like one that was found recently at West Row in Suffolk still in its original scabbard (fig. 20). This scabbard consisted of flat laths of hazel wood glued together and surrounded by thin metal sheets which were both functional and decorative. The handle of the rapier was missing but it was probably of bone or horn, and the whole can give us some idea of the splendid equipment of the Middle Bronze Age warrior.

It is difficult, however, to relate the Middle Bronze Age warrior and his magnificent bronze weapons to the evidence that we have for the economy and settlements of the Middle Bronze Age people in East Anglia as a whole. They appear to have lived mainly by stock breeding, with some crop raising and hunting to supplement their diet. Their house types are unknown and they may merely have lived in temporary shelters, although the amount of material at Mildenhall Fen suggests that there was fairly continuous settlement there. Another factor which suggests that they lived in larger and more permanent communities than we might otherwise believe is the development of extensive Urnfield cemeteries which would presuppose a large settled community close by.

LATE BRONZE AGE HOARDS

Although the settlement evidence in the

Early and Middle Bronze Age is scanty, it is very rich compared with the material evidence from the last phase of the Bronze Age, which consists solely of hoards of metal objects. This period begins about 1000 B.C. and lasts until the arrival of iron-using people from the Continent in the sixth century B.C. The main cultural traits continued unbroken throughout the Middle and Late Bronze Ages, and the line between the two is drawn at the time when the use of bronze increased and not only weapons but tools began to be made of metal which had previously been very precious. Well over forty founders' hoards (p. 38) have been found in East Anglia and it seems that the production of tools and weapons was now in the hands of itinerant smiths who, carrying their raw materials with them, supplied the needs of the population. Whereas Middle Bronze Age styles tended to be entirely local in their development, the Late Bronze Age saw the introduction of foreign forms and the consequent appearance of new weapon types. Foreign influence was also responsible for an improvement in techniques, notably the introduction of the *cire perdue* (lost wax) process of bronze casting. This method involves making a model of the desired object in wax, encasing it in clay all except for a small hole, and then baking it. This means that the wax melts and escapes, leaving its impression in the clay which is then filled with molten bronze, enabling much more elaborate shapes to be made.

An increasing number of weapons was made throughout the Late Bronze Age; the native rapier of the Middle Bronze Age was replaced by the leaf-shaped sword which was adapted for both slashing and thrusting. Socketed axes which were simpler to haft were introduced, and examples of these can be seen from the Feltwell Fen hoard (fig. 21). Leaf-shaped spearheads were made with a rivet for hafting, and the native Middle Bronze Age socketed spearhead with loops below the blade was developed so that the once-useful loops became purely decorative (fig. 21).

Among the tools which were now made are socketed chisels, gouges (Feltwell), hammers, awls and knives (Thorndon) (fig. 21). Socketed and tanged sickles have also been found and toilet articles for personal use begin to make their appearance; tweezers and razors are among the most common objects. Bridle-bits indicate that horses were being harnessed and this supports the suggestion that ploughs were introduced and heavy land began to be cultivated.

Also at this late period East Anglia seems to share in the general Bronze Age prosperity which had first shown itself in the Wessex culture almost a thousand years earlier. Gold ornaments have been found in some numbers, both in founders' hoards, as the gold foil in the Feltwell hoard, or as separate deposits. Perhaps the richest of these is the group of gold objects from Caister-by-Yarmouth (fig. 22) where two bracelets and two penannular objects (perhaps cloak fasteners) were found; these were probably made in Ireland and may have been awaiting shipment to the Continent when they were concealed. Similar objects have been found at Sporle in Suffolk and at Reepham, Fulmodeston Common and Melton Constable in Norfolk, and all appear to have been manufactured in Ireland during the seventh century B.C., a very late phase of the Late Bronze Age.

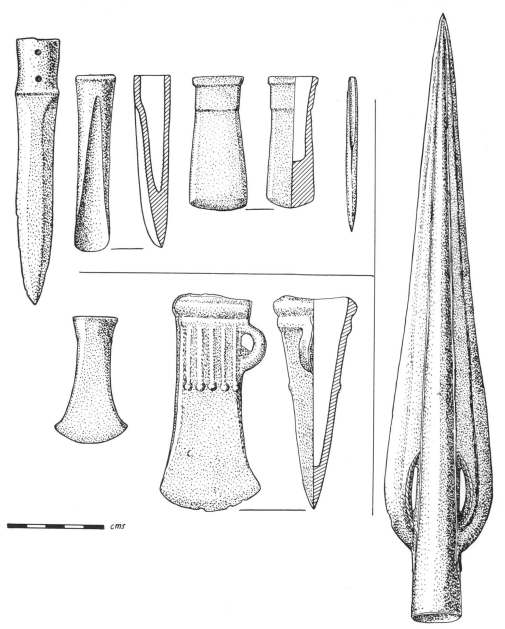

Fig. 21 *Late Bronze Age implements and weapons: (above) socketed knife, gouge, hammer and awl from the Thorndon hoard; (below) socketed chisel and axe from the Feltwell Fen hoard; (right) spearhead from Burwell Fen*

From Geldeston Hall in Norfolk come the remains of sheet-gold collars which appear to be of German origin. Thus it seems possible that at this late period of the Late Bronze Age East Anglia was being drawn into a trading position between east and west which boosted its wealth. Remains of an Irish bronze cauldron found at Ipswich also support this view.

A few intimations of the disruption of this peaceful way of life may be inferred from the occasional object of Hallstatt (European Early Iron Age) type found in East Anglia; notably a sword scabbard chape from Lakenheath. Casual raids from across the North Sea seem to have become quite frequent during the seventh century B.C., culminating in a full-scale invasion from northern France and the Low Countries and the arrival in the British Isles of the first iron-using peoples.

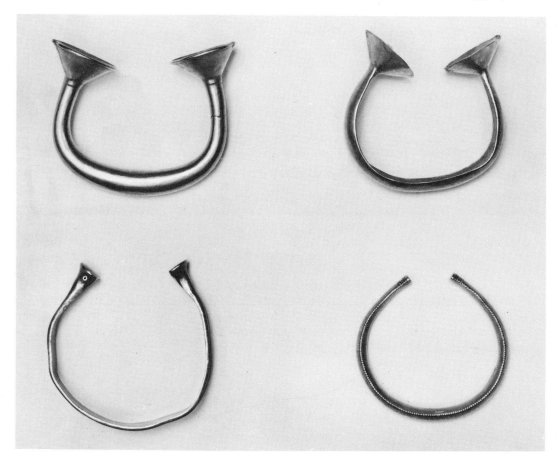

Fig. 22 *Gold cloak fasteners and bracelets from Caister-by-Yarmouth*

6 New Invaders from the Continent: The Iron Age

The arrival of people of an iron-using culture had an immediate and far-reaching effect on the native Bronze Age population of the British Isles. During the last phase of the Bronze Age (at the end of the seventh century B.C.) objects of undoubtedly continental Iron Age type have been found. These have been interpreted as the remains of occasional raids on the east coast and the Wash by people from the Continent who penetrated up the rivers but who did not come or settle in numbers large enough to leave a permanent mark on the indigenous culture. They may have been individual adventurers out for personal gain, or perhaps the vanguard of people who were to come later, spying out the land with a view to subsequent settlement. These sporadic raids were followed at some time in the sixth century B.C. by a much more intensive settlement by small groups of Iron Age farmers who came from various areas of north-west Europe and brought with them the equipment and economy of the *Late Hallstatt* culture.

The earliest iron-using culture on the Continent is known as Hallstatt from the site in Austria where its significance was first recognized. The various phases of the Hallstatt culture were finally superseded by the continental *La Tène* culture which began to appear during the late sixth and early fifth centuries B.C. As the arrival of the Iron Age in Britain was much later than on the Continent, the earliest and purest forms of these cultures do not occur here, and consequently the European terminology cannot be applied to British sites. The Iron Age in Britain is divided into three main phases, A, B and C; *Iron Age A* covers about 250 years from the first arrival of Iron Age settlers in Britain around 550 B.C. until it is displaced or modified by a second and more limited wave of people from the La Tène cultural area which was near the River Marne in northern France. The British Iron Age A is an amalgam of late Hallstatt and some early La Tène characteristics with the culture of the indigenous Bronze Age population. The people of the Iron Age A culture co-existed with the later *Iron Age B* invaders and even the final Iron Age immigration of *Iron Age C* peoples in the first century B.C., and probably maintained their own life and culture until the arrival of the Romans in A.D. 43. At the same time, not all the native Bronze Age people were absorbed or even influenced by the Hallstatt immigrants and for a considerable time there must have been Iron Age A and Bronze Age people living, if not side by side, at least in adjacent territories.

The chronological divisions are somewhat misleading: Iron Age A developed in the sixth century B.C. through the mingling of the Hallstatt, early La Tène and native Bronze Age traits, and existed in places until the beginning of the Christian era; Iron Age B arrived with the

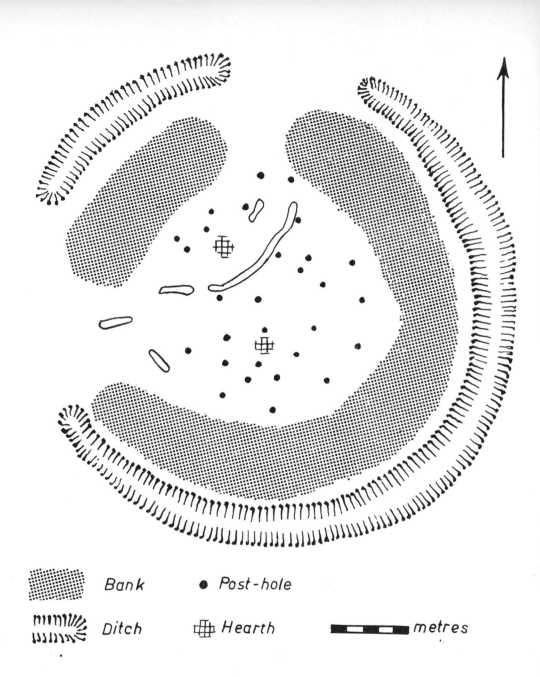

Bank

Post-hole

Ditch

Hearth

metres

Fig. 23 *Plan of Iron Age A house, West Harling*

46

new wave of immigrants about 300 B.C. but did not necessarily affect all the older populations, and finally, at the beginning of the first century B.C., the Iron Age C peoples, the *Belgae,* arrived from north Gaul and the Low Countries and established themselves mainly in south-east England.

Very pronounced regional differences emerged during the Iron Age, and by the time the Romans arrived, Britain had been organized on a tribal basis for some hundred years.

IRON AGE A PEOPLE: THE WEST HARLING GROUP

In the sixth century B.C. small groups of Late Hallstatt farmers began to arrive in Britain and to look for land. They settled over much of southern England where they built isolated farmsteads which have left considerably more remains than any buildings from earlier periods.

An example of early contact between the Hallstatt invaders and the native Bronze Age population can be seen in the sixth-century site at West Harling in Norfolk. This settlement lies in the breckland, on Micklemoor Hill, on the south bank of the River Thet. The site seems to have consisted of two buildings, one circular and one oval, which were in occupation at the same time, as well as a rectangular structure which was built at a rather later date and may have served as an outhouse.

All that remains of the buildings are their ground plans which show a number of post holes within an area enclosed by a bank and ditch (fig. 23). The two earlier buildings—one 72 feet in diameter, the other 94×106 feet were built of upright timber posts which supported thatched roofs whose eaves rested on the top of the bank. The ditch may have served as an eavesdrip. The true construction of the building is very difficult to work out from the ground plan because the post holes do not seem to form any regular pattern and also because of the problem of roofing such a large area. One reconstruction suggests that the circular house was not roofed over completely but that it had a central open area surrounded by a roofed corridor, with entrances into the building through the gaps in the bank and ditch.

The rectangular house was of a different, *sleeper beam,* construction. By this method, beams for the foundations are laid in trenches in the ground and upright posts for the walls and roof jointed into them. The rectangular building at West Harling seems to be a complete innovation; what little evidence we have for Bronze Age buildings in Britain suggests that the round house was the usual form and that this was the tradition which continued into the Iron Age. Rectangular buildings seem to have been unknown to the native British population and their plan may have been introduced into East Anglia by the earliest Iron Age A invaders.

The inhabitants of West Harling mainly bred cattle, sheep and horses, but they supplemented their diet by hunting wild pig, red deer, beaver and crane. Saddle querns for grinding grain indicate that they grew cereals, probably barley, wheat, rye and spelt. Evidence for this comes not from this site but from other areas, mainly further south, where storage pits for grain were dug into the ground; these were not used at West Harling where grain was stored in pottery or wooden jars in the houses. Woollen cloth was woven (fig. 24) and hides

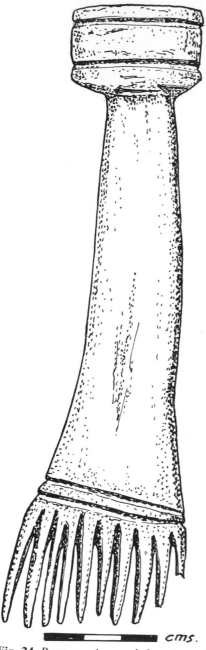

Fig. 24 *Bone weaving comb from Ipswich*

cms.

were worked with flint scrapers. Neither bronze nor iron tools were found, although a handle made of antler implies that metal tools may have been in use. Very few iron tools, however, have been found in East Anglia from any period of the Iron Age; this may be attributable both to the bad preservation properties of the soil and to the poverty of the population.

The most distinctive feature of the finds from West Harling lies in the pottery (fig. 25), which appears to derive from the coarse ware traditions of the Bronze Age. The main element of decoration consists of finger impressions, but there are other features such as incised herringbone patterns, dots or triangles. Some of these features are found on pottery from other sites along the east coast from Yorkshire to Kent, and they illustrate the combination of Iron Age and Bronze Age traits which is characteristic of the development of Iron Age A in the British Isles. Other traits such as the continuance of flint working and the use of round houses also reflect Bronze Age survivals.

West Harling pottery is also found in a number of cremation burials in East Anglia (fig. 26). At Warborough Hill, Stiffkey, on the north Norfolk coast a round barrow between 40 and 50 feet in diameter and surrounded by a ditch contained multiple cremations with remains of a bipartite bowl of West Harling type; and in Suffolk, a site at Creeting St. Mary has produced a cremation in a flat grave, the ashes contained in a tripartite urn decorated with plain cordons. Also from south-east Suffolk, some sherds from Darmsden exhibit the same decorative forms as West Harling pottery, although the pottery itself is distinctive because

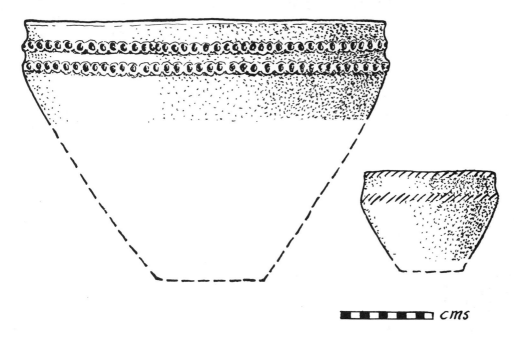

Fig. 25 *Iron Age A pottery from West Harling*

of its haematite-covered surface. This may indicate that the populations around the estuaries of the south-east Suffolk rivers were of a different culture from those of north-west Suffolk and south-west Norfolk, as they were in the Late Bronze Age.

THE FENGATE–CROMER GROUP

In the fifth century B.C. the so-called Fengate-Cromer type of pottery was developed by people who lived in Norfolk and along the fen edges. Nothing is known of these people except their pottery which is generally finer than the West Harling ware although it does occasionally incorporate West Harling traits in its later forms. The Fengate-Cromer pottery of the first half of the fifth century B.C. may represent an im-

migration into East Anglia of people from the Netherlands who later mingled with the West Harling people, originating a mixture of pottery styles. Our knowledge of this phase is very slight, with only three sites in Norfolk producing this ware, and none at all in Suffolk.

These two local pottery groups and their associated finds form the basis of our knowledge of the sixth and fifth centuries B.C. in East Anglia. The population consisted of farmers living in round houses, cultivating the soil and breeding domestic animals, supplementing their diet by hunting, clothing themselves in woollen cloth and cremating their dead. Other areas of England have produced richer finds; we know from the so-called *Celtic Fields* that the Iron

49

Age A population ploughed rectilinear patches of ground and it is thought that large-scale cattle ranching took place on the more open downland. It is evident from East Anglia, as elsewhere, that the people had now adopted a much more settled type of life, built more substantial dwellings and relied more on farming than hunting for their livelihood. This economy was to last, in many places, unchanged until Roman times.

IRON AGE B: THE MARNIAN CHIEFTAINS

At the end of the fourth century B.C. a new group of immigrants arrived in eastern England and this marked the

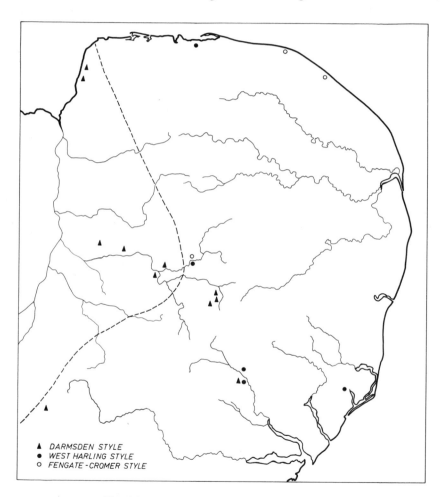

Fig. 26 *Distribution of Early Iron Age pottery*

50

beginning of the Iron Age B phase. These people, from the Marne region of northern France, were chieftains with bands of warriors who imposed themselves as rulers on the native population. Their culture, of the European La Tène type, was essentially warlike in character and it introduced new styles of metalworking to the British Isles. Decorative art on metal objects began to develop a quality and style hitherto unknown. These art styles are very close to their continental La Tène prototypes although in time local variations began to develop. The new arrivals also brought with them their own pottery forms, burial customs and a new method of warfare based on the chariot. The significance of the chariot in the La Tène culture is shown by the number of burials of this period which are accompanied by chariots and horse trappings. These are particularly evident in east Yorkshire, but we also have considerable evidence from East Anglian finds.

THE DARMSDEN GROUP

On arrival the La Tène warriors appear to have established suzerainty over the native population, but shortly afterwards a mingling of the native and immigrant cultures seems to have taken place. In East Anglia during the fourth and third centuries B.C. a type of pottery was in use which was very closely related to the La Tène I pottery of the Continent and yet which displays characteristics suggesting continuity with forms from the earlier Iron Age A. This characteristic Iron Age B pot in East Anglia has recently been named the *Darmsden group* after a site at Darmsden, Suffolk, and is found mainly along the Little Ouse–Waveney valley, but also at a group of

sites in the Thames valley, particularly in the Oxford region (fig. 26). The main feature of the pottery—mainly bowls and jars—is the fine burnished black surface which may be decorated with horizontal grooves or finger-tip impressions, although more usually it is plain.

No distinct culture can be assigned to the people using this type of pottery, although on balance it seems likely that Iron Age A forms continued and that the only intrusive element was the pottery. Certain of the characteristic features associated with sites on which Darmsden pottery has been found seem to be a continuation of Iron Age A traditions, notably a bone industry which still seems to be producing weaving combs, spindle whorls and 'scoops' or spoons, made from tibia, of Iron Age A form; and also the presence at practically all the sites of large storage pits, the common feature of Iron Age A outside East Anglia. One of the more unusual features of the Darmsden sites is the frequent association of the pottery with rectangular huts; at Hinderclay in Suffolk a rectilinear timber structure was discovered and at Calke Wood, Wattisfield, three post holes in a straight line and an adjacent clay floor give definite evidence for a rectilinear structure. Similar huts have been found at Feltwell and Snarehill in Norfolk. On the other hand, a round hut has been found on a Darmsden site at Esher in Surrey. It may be that there was no exclusive house type associated with the Darmsden group and that the finds of rectangular houses in East Anglia are purely fortuitous; at West Harling in the earlier period, for instance, the presence of round and rectangular huts may indicate the beginnings of an East Anglian tradition of mixed house types.

The Marnian chieftains did not settle and take over the native populations entirely unopposed. They penetrated into eastern England along the east coast rivers, and in East Anglia settled on the dry and fertile land along the fen edges. Resistance on the part of the Iron Age A peoples is shown by the construction of defences in various strategic positions along lines of communication; they were built on whatever rising ground was provided by the rolling East Anglian countryside and are the lowland equivalent of the magnificent hillforts found in the more hilly areas of Britain.

On the Gog Magog Hills in Cambridgeshire, just on the edge of our region, Wandlebury fort was constructed to guard the approaches to the Icknield Way. During the third century B.C. a roughly circular area about 15 acres in extent was surrounded by a ditch and an earth-and-timber rampart. The threat which caused the fort to be built evidently did not last long, for when the timbers of the rampart began to decay they were not replaced and the defences fell into disrepair. This probably represents the time when the La Tène invaders had consolidated their hold, and resistance on the part of the natives was futile.

Other evidence for forts or camps comes from Norfolk where three sites were defended by single ramparts and ditches. The fort at South Creake lies on the 200-foot contour which is almost as high as it could be in Norfolk, but the other two sites, at Narborough (on the River Nar adjacent to the Icknield Way) and at Tasburgh (beside a tributary of the River Wensum), both lie on lower ground.

Fig. 27 *Iron sword from Shouldham*

LA TÈNE BURIALS

While these forts were being raised against them, the Marnians were consolidating their hold around the edges of the fenland where a number of rich burials testify to their permanent settlement. The equipment in these graves is of purely La Tène type, which suggests that it belonged to a people who had not yet merged with local populations but who were maintaining their culture and traditions as they had been on the Continent.

At Mildenhall a chariot grave was discovered in the nineteenth century; the burial contained a male skeleton with his equipment—an iron sword, an iron axe and a gold torc—and the skeletons of two horses. At Icklingham, Suffolk, a child was buried wearing a ribbed bronze bracelet, and at Shouldham, Norfolk, a man was interred with an iron sword across his chest (fig. 27). This sword was of a specifically La Tène type with an anthropomorphic handle and is paralleled by a stray find from Hertford Warren, near Bury St. Edmunds, which might originally have been part of a grave group. The most splendid burial lies on the edge of our area at Newnham Croft, Cambridgeshire. This is a very rich chariot burial of a middle-aged man wearing a cast-bronze arm-ring and a bronze brooch decorated with knobs of shell. Horse trappings included a bronze pony cap with 'dingle-dangles', a form of ceremonial headgear known from other Marnian burials. All these burials and objects seem to date from the late third or early second century B.C. and the burial customs are similar to those practised on the Continent at this time. The material from the graves is of the same style as objects from Yorkshire and northern France, and this implies that art styles and metalworking techniques did not develop local and regional characteristics in the same way as pottery (such as the Darmsden group). Metal equipment in the third and second centuries B.C. belonged to a ruling class who maintained ascendancy over the common people and were sharply distinguished from them both by their use of highly specialized and fine equipment and by their contacts with abroad. It is not until the first century B.C. in East Anglia that the pure La Tène styles were modified by local craftsmen.

The second century B.C. saw a further extension in regionalization and independent development. After the pottery of the Darmsden group developed in the third century B.C., and before intrusive Belgic forms of pottery became common in East Anglia at the end of the first century B.C., individual areas developed their own pottery forms and specific regional groups began to emerge both in East Anglia and elsewhere. This is when the Celtic British tribal system was formed and in East Anglia the people coalesced into the *Iceni* who occupied Norfolk and most of Suffolk and the *Trinovantes* who lived in south-east Suffolk. The tribal chiefs were the descendants of the Marnian warriors, and their subjects were the older native populations of both Iron Age A and Iron Age B cultures. This state of affairs was developing during the last two centuries B.C., and the tribes had finally settled into their first century B.C. form when a new wave of invaders, the Belgae, arrived from the Continent, settled in south-east England and organized their own tribal system. This arrival heralds the beginning of Iron Age C.

The arrival of the Belgae during the first century B.C. introduces for the first time a historical people whose names and deeds are recorded in Roman texts and whose leaders emerge as recognizable men with names and characters of their own. The Belgae arrived in south-east England from northern France and the Low Countries in several successive invasions, although finds of Belgic coins from the middle of the second century B.C. onwards suggest that the invasions began with sporadic attacks by small groups of people, rather in the same way as the Hallstatt people first arrived in England during the Late Bronze Age.

Once the Belgae had settled in England they spread rapidly in the south and in the area immediately north of the Thames; but they did not penetrate into East Anglia where the non-Belgic Iceni and Trinovantes lived. In these two tribal areas the life of the people remained little different from that of the previous two centuries and Belgic influence infiltrated only very gradually. One of the first signs of their influence is shown by the introduction of coinage into East Anglia. Before the arrival of the

Fig. 28 *Reverse of Icenian Silver coin from Oxnead, decorated with a stylized horse*

Belgae, Britain had had a non-monetary economy and the second-century B.C. Belgic coins are the first to be found in this country. During the first century B.C. a coinage was adopted throughout the country after the Belgic pattern. Early Icenian coins were copied from Gallo-Belgic coins and bear a male head (supposedly that of Apollo) on one side and a disjointed horse on the other. A few of these coins, minted in the first half of the first century B.C., have been found from East Anglia, but more are known from the second half of that century (fig. 28). Both gold and silver coins were issued by the Iceni, and during the first half of the first century A.D. silver coins inscribed with the names of tribal kings were minted. Many of these have been found in coin hoards in both Norfolk and Suffolk. The deposition of coin hoards in the ground—that is, the hiding of one's valuables—always indicates that the population is undergoing some trouble or disturbance; the first-century hoards in East Anglia are probably the result of Belgic threats along the borders of the Icenian and Trinovantian territory, and the ultimate conquest of south-east Suffolk by the Belgae.

THE BELGAE IN SUFFOLK

At the beginning of the first century A.D. the Trinovantian capital Camulodunum (Colchester) was captured by Dubnovellaunus of Kent and was subsequently taken over by another Belgic monarch, Cunobelinus, king of the *Catuvellauni* of Hertfordshire and Essex. Colchester was adopted as the capital of the Catuvellauni and became one of the most important settlements in England during both this and the Roman period. Typical Belgic wheel-made pottery is found in southern Suffolk from this time onwards and settlements were established in areas hitherto uninhabited because of the unsuitability of the Boulder Clay for agriculture. The Belgae were more capable of cultivating heavy lands than had been the earlier settlers of East Anglia and their penetration of south Suffolk was not confined to the light soils of the river valleys. Places such as Long Melford, Sudbury and Burgh near Woodbridge seem to have been Belgic settlements, and cemeteries are also known, for instance the two at Boxford.

The Boxford cemeteries, only 500 yards apart and roughly contemporary, were in use during the first half of the first century when the Catuvellauni were consolidating their position in south-east Suffolk and probably also attempting to push northwards into Icenian lands. All the burials were cremations in urns concealed in flat graves, and forty-three Belgic wheel-made pots were found (fig. 29). A few metal objects were buried with the dead, the most notable being bronze brooches and a bronze toilet set of Roman type which suggest that Roman influence was already being felt by the Belgae. These two cemeteries probably represent several family groups who were perhaps moving northwards to settle the fringes of Icenian territory; one child was buried in the cemetery, but the majority of graves seemed to contain the bones of adults, at least three of whom had reached the age of thirty-five—a fairly high age for that period.

ICENIAN DEFENCES AGAINST THE BELGAE

The settlement of the Catuvellauni right on the southern borders of the Iceni obviously threatened the security of Norfolk and Suffolk, and the non-Belgic

cms.

Fig. 29 *Belgic cremation jars from the Boxford cemetery*

tribe responded by trying to defend its frontiers. Clare Camp in Suffolk was probably built at this time when several rings of banks and ditches were thrown up around a defended area. The defences at Wandlebury were repaired at the end of the first century B.C. or the beginning of the first century A.D. and permanent occupation took place within its walls. These two earthworks were border fortresses against the Belgae, and other camps, Warham, Holkham and Wighton in north Norfolk, and Thetford in the breckland, may have been built as refuges, all, except Thetford, well away from the border.

At the time of the Roman conquest of Britain in A.D. 43 the Iceni of Norfolk were being threatened very strongly by the Catuvellauni who, as well as pressing ever more powerfully on their southern frontier, may also have settled in south breckland. Several cremation burials containing exclusively Belgic material have been found in the breckland, for instance at Snailwell near Newmarket

and at Elveden near Thetford, and these could be the graves of Belgic warriors already living on the very fringes of Icenian territory.

Although the Iceni were ready to repel any attack from the Belgae, their culture was influenced by Belgic traits. Wheel-made pottery began to be copied in Icenian wares, various Belgic decorative motives were adopted by the Iceni, and the whole concept of a coinage inscribed with a chieftain's name was entirely a Belgic characteristic. But the Belgae had not actually invaded East Anglia when the arrival of the Romans gave the Iceni a momentary respite by forcing the Catuvellauni to defend their territories to the south.

ICENIAN RICHES: METAL HOARDS FROM THE FIRST CENTURY B.C.

The material remains of the Iceni from the first century B.C. and the first half of the first century A.D. present a picture of a poverty-stricken people; there is a dearth of all tools and weapons of either bronze or iron, very few coins are met with outside coin hoards, there is little sign of extensive settlement and, compared with the Belgae, the Iceni were both economically weak and culturally backward. This is to some extent confirmed by the readiness with which the Iceni absorbed cultural traditions from their more advanced neighbours to the south, but it is, on the other hand, contradicted by a very large number of bronze, silver and gold decorative objects which were made in East Anglia during the first century B.C. These have either been found as hoards or as stray deposits hidden in the ground for safe-keeping; the hoards seem to represent the stock of goldsmiths as they generally contain both scrap metal for melting down and re-working, and also articles ready for sale. The ornaments are of incredible sumptuousness and high-quality workmanship, and must have been made for tribal rulers of very considerable wealth who were anxious to display their wealth and power by adorning both themselves and their horses.

Both types of object—horse trappings with elaborate enamelled designs, and neck ornaments and bracelets with embossed decoration—remind one of the finds buried in the lavish Marnian graves of earlier centuries, and the ornamentation applied to them is a local British development of the earlier La Tène art styles. It is probable that they belonged to the descendants of the Marnian chieftains who took over the leadership of the native population in the third and second centuries B.C. and transformed the Iron Age A peoples of East Anglia into the tribes of the Iceni and Trinovantes. The subject peoples—the common people of the tribe—seem to have continued their Iron Age A way of life, farming the lighter soils and living in West Harling type farmsteads, while their rulers amassed great wealth which they displayed ostentatiously. Never before have we seen so clearly from the archaeological records the division between the ruling and ruled.

TORCS

Objects of personal adornment are by far the most splendid things found in the East Anglian hoards, and are mainly in the form of heavy metal neck ornaments known as *torcs*. In all, seventy neck rings have been found in East Anglia, all but five of them from north-west Norfolk. Sixty-one come from the amazingly rich hoards of bronze, tin and precious metal found at Snettisham; fifty-eight whole or fragmentary torcs were found in five hoards discovered in 1948 and 1950, and three were found on separate occasions in 1964 and 1968. The other west Norfolk torcs come from Bawsey, Sedgeford and North Creake, and the ones from outside Norfolk were found at Ipswich in 1968 and 1970.

First-century B.C. torcs may be divided into four broad categories: *loop-terminal, ring-terminal, buffer-terminal* and *tubular* torcs.

The simplest of all loop-terminal torcs consist of a single rod of metal, bronze, tin or gold, twisted into a barley-sugar shape and then formed into a circle to encase the throat. Each end of the rod is then bent back to form a loop. These, and a more complicated form of loop-terminal torc made by twisting two or more metal rods together, are by far the most common type and over fifty of them, made of gold alloy, bronze or tin, were found at Snettisham, mainly in a fragmentary condition as they had been cut up ready for melting down and re-use. A gold loop-terminal torc from Snettisham (fig. 30) had one of its loops threaded with a gold split ring which was probably used for securing the torc when it was being worn. Similar loop-terminal neck rings are known from Bawsey in west Norfolk and Ipswich in Suffolk.

The five loop-terminal torcs found at Ipswich in 1968 are all of gold alloyed with silver and a little copper (an alloy called electrum), and four of them are unique in that they have decorated terminals. The embossed curvilinear decoration is embellished with chasing and engraving (fig. 31) and is of a type developed from La Tène prototypes. The torcs are dated to about 75 B.C.

The same type of decoration is seen on the ring-terminal torcs from Snettisham, North Creake and Bawsey. These consist of a number of strands of gold or electrum wire twisted together and terminating in a hollow ring which is

Fig. 30 *Loop-terminal torc from the Snettisham Treasure*

Fig. 31 *Decorated loop-terminal torc from Ipswich*

soldered onto them by means of a gold collar. The only complete example in the British Isles is the magnificent electrum torc from Snettisham (fig. 32) consisting of eight strands, each of eight wires, which have been twisted together like a rope. Each end of this rope is fitted onto a beautifully decorated ring.

These ring-terminal torcs are thought to have been made at a rather later date than the loop-terminal torcs, but still well within the first century B.C.

Tubular torcs and buffer-terminal torcs are also known from the Snettisham hoards. They seem to be of continental inspiration although both types were probably made in this country, and they are very clear examples of the contact that was maintained between the ruling classes in England and their La Tène homeland. The Snettisham hoards contained many other precious objects such as rings, coins, miscellaneous fragments of sheet gold and bronze, and bracelets, one of which shows very high quality workmanship and was probably made by the same craftsman who made the ring-terminal torc (fig. 33).

The splendour of the great gold torcs from these finds suggests either that they were worn by very important people or that they adorned statues of gods as a sign of their power. Some of them were of considerable weight—the ring-terminal torc from Snettisham weighed almost $2\frac{1}{2}$ lb—and must have been too heavy for comfort, but all the torcs were carefully finished on their inner surface as if to prevent their rubbing against the skin, and were of a suitable size for wearing. It is mentioned in classical authors that Boudicca, the queen of the Iceni at the time of their revolt against the Romans in A.D. 61, habitually wore a gold neck ornament as a sign of rank but the numbers that have been found and the discrepancy in their styles and materials suggest that torcs were worn by whoever could afford them and not exclusively by the ruling house.

HORSE TRAPPINGS AND OTHER EQUIPMENT

Another method by which the Iceni displayed their wealth was by decking their horses and chariots with elaborate equipment, usually of bronze decorated with relief ornament or inlaid with enamels. Bridle bits are among the most commonly decorated horse trappings and a pair found at Ringstead in Norfolk

are as fine as any from first-century
Britain. They consist of three links of
cast bronze (fig. 34) with iron side rings
covered in bronze; they appear never to
have been used. A similar bit has been
found from Swanton Morley, also in Norfolk, which, it has been calculated, was

Fig. 32 *Ring-terminal torc from the Snettisham
Treasure*

Fig. 33 *Design on the bracelet from the
Snettisham Treasure*

60

suitable for harnessing a pony thirteen hands high. All three bits are paralleled by objects from Yorkshire and have very close affinities with the horse trappings of the earlier Marnians. A fragmentary bridle bit was found from Snettisham, and decorated linchpins from chariot wheels have been found from Marham and Thornham, both in Norfolk. Other finds have included decorative bronze plates from shields, strap ends, and rivets which would all have made up part of an Icenian warrior's equipment.

The tradition was maintained throughout most of the next century, and first-century horse trappings, including enamelled harness mounts, have been found from Santon Downham and Westhall, both in Suffolk. We can imagine that when the Iceni came face to face with the Roman army in A.D. 61 and finally lost their independence, their leaders, at least, were a splendid group

Fig. 34 *Pair of bridle-bits from Ringstead*

61

ostentatiously wearing gold and silver ornaments and driving chariots glittering with bronze and enamelwork. If the rest of the archaeological evidence is to be believed, the Icenian chieftains must have led an ill-assorted crew into battle— including groups of Iron Age A people who struggled to gain a subsistence living from the soil and who were hardly wealthy enough to own an iron sickle, never mind a gold torc.

CENTRES OF POPULATION

The concentration of gold objects in north-west Norfolk might suggest that the Icenian headquarters were situated there, but no evidence has been found for any significant settlement sites in the area. The only gold hoard from outside the region (the five loop-terminal torcs from Ipswich) comes from a part of East Anglia that is particularly sparse in Iron Age finds and therefore seems unlikely to have been the centre of a rich nobility. Four of the Ipswich torcs were unfinished at the time of their deposition, so it seems probable that they were made nearby, perhaps at the order of a local lord. But no remains of either jeweller's workshop or settlement are known.

The greatest concentration of finds is in the breckland and it seems most probable that, as in earlier periods, this area supported the largest number of people, although a secondary centre of population grew up near present-day Norwich which, in the Roman period, was developed into the cantonal capital, Venta Icenorum.

7 The Roman Period

When the Roman invading armies set foot on English soil in A.D. 43 the Iceni of East Anglia were more likely to have welcomed than resisted their arrival. The pressure of the Catuvellauni against the Icenian southern border was immediately relieved when the Belgic tribe found itself face to face with the Roman invaders and the Iceni must have felt that their independence was assured. The Catuvellauni were promptly overcome by the Romans, the capital of England was established at Colchester, and the Essex and south-east Suffolk area (once Trinovantian territory) became the most rapidly and intensively Romanized area of Britain. The Iceni, on the other hand, were not a conquered and subject people but were allied to Rome as a tribute state or kingdom, with a treaty of friendship between the two peoples and, in theory at least, a reasonably favoured position.

But the peaceful treaty was not to last

long. In A.D. 47 the Coritani of the midlands rose in revolt against Roman rule and were joined by their eastern neighbours, the Iceni. The failure of this revolt resulted in the Romans taking a somewhat firmer line with the Iceni although they still were not placed fully under the Roman yoke. The Romans probably removed the Icenian king, the 'Saemu' of early first-century Icenian coins, and replaced him by Prasutagus, whose death in A.D. 60 brought about the next and final clash between the Iceni and Rome.

The first decade or so of Roman rule in England seems to have left little impression on the Iceni, although even at this early stage there is some evidence for contacts with the Romanized south in the appearance in East Anglia of objects of obviously Roman manufacture or affinity. Some such may have been acquired by the Iceni as gifts from their allies, notably the bronze bowl which was found together with two mid-first-century Roman brooches at Lakenheath, and the bronze bowl and cauldron from Swanton Morley in the Wensum valley. But the degree of contact must have been small and the very slight Romanization of the area at this time sets the scene for subsequent centuries when East Anglia, although by then completely within the Roman Empire, remained a backward community consisting essentially of the native Iron Age rural populations with an economy very similar to that

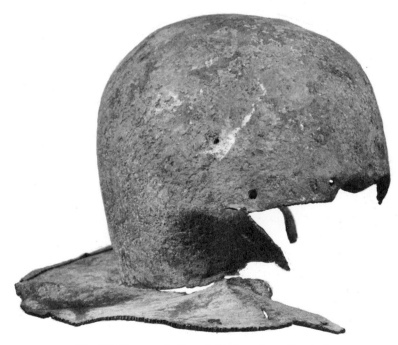

Fig. 35 *Roman gladiatorial helmet from Hawkedon*

of the pre-Roman period, accepting some aspects of Roman life but never becoming as completely and successfully Romanized as much of the rest of lowland England.

THE REVOLT OF BOUDICCA, A.D. 61

As dependent monarch, Prasutagus was not allowed to bequeath his kingdom as he wished, and he attempted to reconcile claims of family and of Rome by leaving half his kingdom to the Emperor Nero, and the other half to be divided between his two daughters. This proved an unsatisfactory solution as the Roman administrators appear to have behaved with unparalleled ferocity, extorting payments in cash and kind and even going so far as to rape Prasutagus's daughters and to flog his widow, Boudicca. This was the sign for the great uprising of A.D. 61 when smouldering resentment of Roman treatment flared into open revolt and the Iceni, joined by the Trinovantes of south-east Suffolk, attacked and captured Camulodunum (Colchester), destroying the town and massacring its inhabitants. Verulamium (St. Albans) and Londinium were exposed to the same treatment before the Roman legions could return from a campaign in Anglesey, engage the Iceni in pitched battle and finally defeat them—probably in Northamptonshire.

Some of the objects looted by the Iceni in their raids found their way to East Anglia where they were buried for safety, probably to protect them from the subsequent Roman punitive raids. At Honingham in Norfolk, and Lakenheath in Suffolk, hoards of mid-first-century Roman coins were concealed, and at Hockwold, Norfolk, a group of five silver wine cups were buried at the edge of the fens. Three of these were very highly decorated with vine, ivy and acanthus leaves, but their handles and pedestal bases had been wrenched off and all five were obviously regarded as scrap metal. They were very probably looted from Camulodunum, as was a bronze helmet which has recently been discovered at Hawkedon in Suffolk. The helmet (fig. 35) is of greater size and weight than the normal first-century legionary helmet and may have been a piece of gladiatorial armour. It is unlikely that the helmet could have reached Hawkedon from anywhere other than Colchester, the nearest Roman settlement with an amphitheatre where gladiatorial contests would have been held. Its massive size and shining appearance no doubt recommended it to the Icenian soldiers while they were devastating the city.

The Northamptonshire battle heralded the end of the kingdom of the Iceni—the tribe was punished by an appalling campaign of retribution, the countryside ravaged, buildings razed to the ground and the population either put to the sword or deported wholesale to the previously unpopulated areas of the fens where an elaborate drainage system was to establish the area as an Imperial agricultural estate.

This campaign of retribution, which was so severe that its instigator (Paulinus, the Governor of Britain) was recalled to Rome by the central government, had the effect of slowing down still further the process of Romanization in East Anglia. As we have seen, before the rebellion of Boudicca the East Anglian countryside was hardly affected by the settlement of Romans along its frontiers, although coinage, pottery and jewellery were finding their way into Icenian territory and there was certainly an awareness of a higher culture beyond the borders—in much the same way as the Belgic Catuvellauni had influenced the Iceni in pre-Roman days. Now, in the period immediately following the rebellion, the hand of Rome lay more heavily upon the population; an administrative centre was set up at Venta Icenorum (Caistor-by-Norwich) and connected by road with Camulodunum; Roman organization and government were moving into East Anglia, which during the next 200 years or so developed, albeit more slowly than elsewhere in England, its own form of Romano-British culture.

ROMANIZATION AND UNREST

Once the Boudiccan revolt had been sufficiently punished the Roman army was withdrawn and East Anglia was left to a peaceful existence. During the second and third centuries the countryside gradually became Romanized; Roman material objects and traditions percolated through the community; agricultural methods were improved; large landowners built themselves farmhouses (*villas*) on the Roman pattern; the road system was extended and towns were established for the first time, either as administrative centres like Venta Icenorum, or as trading ports like Caister-by-Yarmouth. Industry prospered, local kiln sites produced most of the pottery needed in the area, and iron smelting was practised in west Norfolk.

The peace was perhaps not entirely unbroken, for towards the end of the second century the number of coin hoards—always a sign of troubled times —increased quite sharply and continued to rise throughout the third century; there are thirteen coin hoards dated to the third quarter of the third century from Norfolk alone. By the end of that century the region was being harassed by Saxon pirates who infested the North Sea and English Channel and constantly threatened the coast. A chain of fortresses, commonly known as the *forts of the Saxon Shore,* were erected to protect the countryside from attack; in East Anglia they consisted of Branodunum (Brancaster), on the north-west Norfolk coast, Burgh Castle, in north-east Suffolk, and the now totally destroyed Walton Castle near Felixstowe. The fourth century saw the continued occupation of town and countryside in East Anglia, but the coast suffered ever increasing barbarian attacks, culminating in 367 A.D. with the great attack by the Picts, Scots and Saxons. Their ravages were repaired by Count Theodosius, who supplemented the Saxon Shore forts by signal stations such as those at Thornham in Norfolk and Corton in Suffolk and garrisoned them with barbarian mercenary soldiers, *foederati.*

FOURTH- AND FIFTH-CENTURY HOARDS: MILDENHALL TREASURE

During the late fourth and early fifth centuries many valuable objects were buried in East Anglia. Coin hoards were hidden in increasingly large numbers as a result not only of the Saxon attacks but also of the ever-present inflation and the almost total breakdown of the Roman Empire's monetary economy. A hoard from Little Bealing, Suffolk, consisted of about 500 coins mostly from the reign of the Emperor Theodosius (A.D. 379–395); an earlier fourth-century hoard from Freston near Ipswich contained 3100 Constantian coins and another large fourth-century hoard was hidden at Thetford.

Fig. 36 *Silver dish from the Mildenhall Treasure*

Hoards of other precious objects have also been found, notably at Mildenhall where a collection of silver bowls, plates, goblets, ladles and spoons (fig. 36) was concealed at the end of the fourth century or the beginning of the fifth century. All but one of the objects seem to have been made during the fourth century, many of them probably in Romano-British workshops, although some seem to have been imported from the Continent. The general appearance and composition of the collection suggests that it was not a single table service but a number of pieces accumulated throughout the fourth century by a family of wealthy East Anglian landowners who may already have been Christian—some of the spoons are decorated with Christian symbols. The treasure not only enabled the owner to serve his dinners with unprecedented luxury, it also represented a sound investment and was extremely valuable—the average silver content of all the objects was 95·3 per cent. The East Anglian owner of the Mildenhall treasure was, therefore, both fond of lavish display and a keen businessman who preferred to put his wealth into precious metal rather than to keep it in the increasingly debased and inflated currency. At some time of unrest around A.D. 400 the treasure was buried in a place of safety with the hope that the owner would return for it once the danger was over. But this he failed to do.

Precious objects were not the only things concealed during the fourth century. In the fenland area of north-west Suffolk and south-west Norfolk a number of hoards of pewter vessels have recently been discovered. Cups, bowls and platters have been found from Icklingham and Isleham, both in Suffolk, and Hockwold in Norfolk and, although they are not closely datable, they seem to have been deposited during the fourth century. Some of these hoards, particularly that from Icklingham which contained nine pewter cups and bowls, may have been votive deposits buried, perhaps, to pacify the gods and restore peace and prosperity. This may also have been the reason for the burial of five bronze diadems and twenty-three brooches at Hockwold where they were associated with a Romano-Celtic pagan temple. Whether the reason for these deposits was to protect property or placate the gods, they are a fairly clear indication of the political climate of the times.

THE LAST DECADES OF ROMAN RULE: THE EARLY FIFTH CENTURY

By the early decades of the fifth century Roman Britain was suffering from a decline of central power. The Empire's frontiers on the Continent were under pressure from the barbarians and Rome itself was being threatened by the Goths. As a result, Roman troops were withdrawn from Britain and the first half of the fifth century saw the gradual break-down and decay of Roman administration and economy throughout Britain as a whole. In East Anglia during this time there is evidence for some settlement by an Anglo-Saxon population who were to take over the whole of the region by the second half of the fifth century; the earliest evidence for Teutonic settlers in East Anglia comes from burials in and around the Saxon Shore forts which contain grave goods, both metal objects and pottery, of north German and Low Country types. These first appear at the end of the fourth century and represent the graves of the Germanic *foederati* brought to Britain to defend the coasts. Throughout the first half of the fifth century the number of Teutonic burials increases and heralds the approach of the next great change in East Anglian life when warlike farmers from the Low Countries took over the land and gave East Anglia the name by which it is still known.

THE COUNTRYSIDE

Agriculture remained the basis of the economy of Britain in Roman times as before, and the gradual improvement in farming techniques, together with an extension of agricultural land through clearance and drainage, led to a period of relative prosperity for East Anglia. At first, Iron Age traditions of cultivation and settlement appear to have been maintained, but throughout the second century there was a more conscious imitation of Roman principles and new methods were gradually adopted by the native population. As in previous periods, the main areas of settlement in the Roman period were concentrated along the river valleys of both Norfolk and Suffolk, but the evidence shows that there was more penetration into the higher Boulder Clay regions. This implies both clearance of the thick oak forests and the ability to cultivate the heavy clay soils. West Norfolk was particularly thickly populated, especially in that area lying to the west of Peddars Way which runs along the chalk ridge bordering the fenland. The edges of the fens had always, from Mesolithic times onwards, been favoured areas of settlement, but in the Roman period occupation seems to have spread well into the heart of the fenland itself, which proved to be one of the most fertile areas in the whole of the British Isles.

THE ROMAN FENLAND

During the Iron Age the fenland was an area of marshes and lagoons unsuited to permanent settlement, but some time during the first half of the first century a lowering of sea level made the area more or less habitable. At the same time, Roman engineers began constructing the Car Dyke, a narrow, flat-bottomed waterway very like a modern barge canal, which skirted the southern edge of the fens and formed a connection between Cambridge and Lincoln. The main purpose of the Car Dyke was to act as a second line of communication and supply from the south-east to the north, supplementing or replacing Watling Street. But secondarily, it acted as a partial drainage system for the fens by connecting some of the rivers and thereby accelerating the drying out of the land.

Some settlement appears to have taken place in the fens during the second half of the first century, but it was not until the beginning of the following century that full exploitation of the area began. After the Boudiccan revolt we know that a proportion of the East Anglian population was transported, and it may have been then that the original settlement began. At least the western part of the fenland was Icenian territory and it may be that after the revolt the land was confiscated from the Iceni and turned into an Imperial estate. If the whole area had been owned by a single authority it would account for the elaborate system of drainage and communications which grew up.

The settlement pattern in the Roman fenland was complex, and it was at this time that the village became a factor in East Anglian rural life. During the first period of occupation, at the end of the first century, the most common settlements in the fens were isolated farmsteads surrounded by their own field systems and generally situated about 500 yards from their nearest neighbours. Such isolated buildings were a tradition carried on from Iron Age types such as those at West Harling, but during the second and third centuries the farmsteads began to be grouped into villages which became the dominant form of settlement. The first signs of village organization can be seen in loosely defined groups of two or three farmhouses which sometimes occur during the first and early second centuries and then develop into much more organized units containing a larger number of houses and an associated system of Celtic fields (small square fields probably used for arable purposes) close by. These fields perhaps represent gardens or stockyards belonging to the houses, but there were also larger fields on the outskirts of the villages which, with their droveways and ditches, may be interpreted as cattle runs. The economy of the villagers, therefore, seems to have been based on mixed farming; one of the most important products may have been wool, and the processing of this seems to have developed into a major industry in East Anglia in Roman times.

Most of our evidence for fenland settlement comes from the higher land of the silt fens which lie to the south of the Wash and along the southern and eastern fen edges between the fens proper and the higher chalk lands. There does, however, seem to have been some settlement along the drainage channels and roads which traversed the fenland. Typical of such settlements was the one at Denver Sluice, where the Fen Causeway crossed the River Great Ouse. This road, the most important highway in the fens, ran eastwards from Durobrivae (Water Newton, Northamptonshire) to Caister-by-Yarmouth on the east Norfolk coast and acted as the main link between East Anglia and the Midlands.

A FENLAND SETTLEMENT: HOCKWOLD-CUM-WILTON

Most of our information about fenland settlement comes from field survey and air photography rather than excavation, but one site on the edge of the fens has recently been excavated. This is at Hockwold-cum-Wilton in the Little Ouse valley at the junction of fen and higher land. Two areas were investigated, one a village, the other a villa, and it seems that the villa was the residence of a landowner whose tenants lived in the village. This is a lay-out which we have not seen from other fenland sites where there is a notable lack of villas, although it is more common in the higher lands of East Anglia.

The two sites were occupied during the second century and at least partially into the third century, although there seems to have been some flooding of the area at that time. The village settlement seems to have replaced an earlier Iron Age occupation on the same site and this illustrates the way in which the native Iron Age population modified its culture and began to conform to a more Romanized way of life. The economy of the settlement was predominantly one of stock breeding; the proportions of animal bones which have been found indicate that cattle were the most common animals, closely followed by sheep and horses (for their meat). Pigs, on the other hand, were rather uncommon and this may be the result of the decrease of woodland through more extensive forest clearance. Animals were probably grazed on the lush fenland pastures and the fens were also used as hunting ground for supplementing the food supply—eels, fish and wild fowl were caught and consumed. This site, with its combination of villa and village, is not typical of the more central fenland sites, but it does give evidence for the general economy of the area. It was once suggested that the fenland was the granary of Roman Britain, but this is not borne out by present evidence and, indeed, it is considered very doubtful whether any grain at all was grown at Hockwold.

The flooding which affected the site in the third century is another feature which connects Hockwold with the fenland proper. Evidence from a number of sites, such as Welney where a layer of silt 6 feet thick was deposited in the third century, indicates serious flooding throughout the fenland, possibly the result of a breakdown in the drainage system. By the end of the century, however, the region was once again prosperous, although with a much reduced population which was once more concentrated on the higher land of the silt fens. By A.D. 300 the central fenland was rapidly becoming submerged and many sites show a thick deposit of silt from about this time. This flooding was far more serious than anything suffered earlier in the Roman period. By the middle of the fifth century the fens were completely abandoned and remained uninhabitable until early in the eighth century when sea level began to drop and the land to dry out.

The fenland shows us an interesting attempt at Roman colonization of a region which, although potentially very fertile, was difficult to settle. Drainage of such a large area indicates that some central plan was in operation and this supports the theory that the fens were an Imperial estate. The settlement pattern, on the other hand, does not suggest any organized plan, and it is probable that the inhabitants of native stock developed their own farms and villages, the latter coming into existence as a result of the nature of the terrain. The fenland farmers appear either to have been small tenants or farm labourers on a large estate, although, apart from Hockwold, there is little evidence for the landowners themselves living in the region.

VILLAS

Outside the fenland, one of the main features of Romanization in East Anglia is the growth of villas. These were essentially large farmhouses built on a formalized plan, with rectangular rooms contained in a number of wings around an open court, and were the dwellings of large landowners who controlled sometimes very extensive estates. In some areas of Britain there are large numbers of villas, but in East Anglia villa remains are fairly rare, the greatest number lying beside Peddars Way in north-west Norfolk. Others are known from the Boulder Clay regions where they tend to stand close to the Roman roads, as at Ixworth in Suffolk, or at river crossings, as at Brettenham, Norfolk. The remains of villas in East Anglia suggest that on the whole they were fairly simple half-timbered constructions built on flint foundations, rather than the more extensive and luxurious buildings known from elsewhere in Roman Britain. Both blocks of buildings at Gayton Thorpe, an excavated villa in west Norfolk, were of half-timbering and were occupied from the middle of the second century to the end of the third or beginning of the fourth century. This time span seems to be typical of East Anglian villas; most of them appear to have been built during the second century and to have flourished during that and at least part of the succeeding century. Where sites continue in use after this a distinct lowering of standards can be seen, particularly in the fourth century when building techniques were shoddy, rooms were allowed to fall into decay and, in some cases, rooms originally intended as dwellings were turned over to industrial purposes. This no doubt reflects the restlessness and disturbance of the countryside in the fourth and fifth centuries caused by the Saxon raids; it was at this time that the Saxon Shore forts were founded and coin hoards deposited in ever-increasing numbers. Villas, however, continued to be a factor in the countryside and some may even have taken on a new lease of life when the towns became less popular as residences in the fourth century and absentee landlords returned to the relative safety of the country. It is certain that some villas were occupied into the fifth century, although the withdrawal of Roman troops and the presence of the Anglo-Saxons made the countryside increasingly unsafe.

Among the amenities of a villa in its heyday was the private bath-house, a building of several rooms heated by means of hypocausts and often elaborately decorated. A number of bath-houses have been found in Norfolk and Suffolk, a recently excavated one being at Stonham Aspal in Suffolk (fig. 37) where remains of a half-timbered building with two rooms were found. These consisted of a cold room at the west and a hot room with a hypocaust at the east. Inside, the walls were covered with plaster decorated with geometric patterns in black, red, yellow, green, blue, pink, orange, mauve and grey paint; the floor was covered with *opus signinum* (a smooth surface made of crushed tiles) and there was opaque green glass in the windows. This pleasant building was constructed in the first half of the third century and continued in use throughout

Fig. 37 *Bath-house at Stonham Aspal, hypocaust in background*

the fourth and possibly into the fifth century. Although it had originally been well built and well decorated there was evidence of a drastic lowering of standards in the fourth century corresponding to similar finds elsewhere.

NATIVE SETTLEMENTS

Villas, although the most spectacular remains of the Romano-British countryside, were by no means the commonest form of settlement as they belonged only to the wealthiest and most Romanized members of the community. The rest of the population lived in small native settlements consisting of a number of dwellings clustered together in loosely knit village communities very like those of the fens. The population gained a living by arable farming and stock raising and were probably the serfs or tenants of the villa landowners. The remains of these native settlements are not so easy to find as villas, and little is known about the construction or standard of the dwellings. The clay lands of central East Anglia seem to have been the areas most densely populated by the native peasants, and, while in some cases native villages are found close to a villa (as at Hockwold), they are more often isolated on the heavier, less satisfactory lands away from the centres of villa occupation. The settlements probably consisted of a collection of primitive huts, either rectangular as at Lakenheath or circular as at Great Fakenham in Suffolk, made of wood and clay and with even less use of masonry than in the East Anglian villas. One site, at Wangford in east Suffolk, shows what a native hut must have been like in the fourth century. The hut had a clay

foundation on which lay a floor of oak boards, the walls were of solid daub (clay lump) and the roof of wattle and daub. On the floor was a heap of barley—the staple crop of the peasants. Spelt, bread wheat and oats have been found elsewhere, and animal bones once again show the predominance of cattle, with sheep a close second and pig definitely lagging behind in importance.

INDUSTRIAL DEVELOPMENT

Although East Anglia remained a predominantly agricultural area throughout the Roman period, a few industries developed in the countryside mainly to supply local needs. It is unlikely that any of the goods made in the region were exported to other parts of Britain and industry never reached the scale it achieved elsewhere.

Our information about Roman industries in East Anglia comes only from rather scanty remains, and these are largely in the form of kilns and furnaces.

Small quantities of iron found in the Carstone of north-west Norfolk were smelted on the spot by means of charcoal-fired furnaces, five of which were found at Ashwicken (fig. 38). The furnaces, of the shaft furnace type, were probably about 6 feet high with an internal diameter of about 1 foot and were constructed entirely of clay. They smelted iron by a very inefficient method which allowed 80 per cent of the iron in the ore to find its way into the slag. The refined ore was probably worked on site into tools or weapons to be distributed by itinerant smiths. This primitive and wasteful method of iron smelting is remarkable when compared with the sophisticated Roman methods used elsewhere, such as in the Weald and the Forest of Dean.

Evaporation of sea water to produce salt was practised at Wolferton on the east coast of the Wash and at Denver Sluice on the River Great Ouse; lime kilns have been found at Bolwick Farm, Aylsham in Norfolk, and glass was made

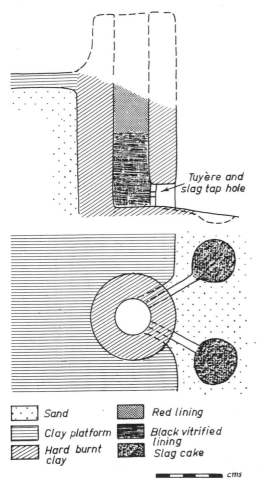

Tuyère and slag tap hole

Sand

Clay platform

Hard burnt clay

Red lining

Black vitrified lining

Slag cake

cms

Fig. 38 *Romano-British iron-smelting furnace at Ashwicken*

at Capel St. Mary, Suffolk, and outside the walls of Caistor-by-Norwich. Tiles were made at Stanningfield, Suffolk. The only industry catering for luxuries seems to have been the manufacture of pewter, a peculiarly English activity which developed in the Mendips about the middle of the third century and was adopted by workers on the fen edges of East Anglia a little later. Pewter ware seems to have been used as a cheap substitute for silver and the objects made in pewter are usually very similar to silver prototypes. A great deal of pewter has been found around the fens and it is assumed that it was made close by, although the actual site of manufacture has not been discovered. Possible centres of pewter working are Brampton in Norfolk, where a stone mould used in the casting of pewter dishes was discovered, and Hockwold in Norfolk, which has produced a pewter ingot.

The discovery of shears and weaving combs supports the theory of the importance of the wool industry to the rural population. It has recently been suggested that Caistor-by-Norwich may have been one of the chief woollen cloth-producing centres in Roman Britain, and the emphasis on sheep farming seems to support this view.

POTTERY MAKING

The East Anglian industry about which we have the most information is pottery making. Although many imported wares —such as Samian ware (*terra sigillata*) from Gaul, or Castor ware from Water Newton—have been found on East Anglian sites it is evident both from the material and from the number of kilns found that much of the local demand

73

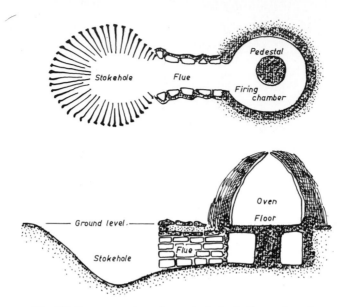

Fig. 39 *Reconstruction of a typical single flue updraught pottery kiln*

was met by the products of local kilns.

By the Roman period, pottery making was no longer a cottage industry with the women of a community making pots by hand and firing them in primitive clamp kilns or bonfires. From the first century onwards most pottery in England was produced in a much more professional way with the aid of the potter's wheel and specially constructed kilns for firing. Far too many kilns have been discovered in East Anglia for them all to be mentioned, but in some cases so many have been found together within a limited area that they must represent the remains of a full-scale pottery industry. The most spectacular groups of kilns are in Suffolk, with the four sites of Grimstone End, Wattisfield, West Stow Heath and Homersfield producing the largest numbers, but there are also similar sites in east Norfolk, at Hevingham for ex-

ample. All the concentrations of kilns are situated on the Boulder Clay lands where both clay for potting and wood for fuel were easily available. The lack of kiln sites in north-west Norfolk is remarkable in view of the number of villas there; it may be that the potteries developed to supply areas which did not receive supplies from further west, and that north-west Norfolk obtained most of its pottery from places such as Water Newton which were accessible across the fens. The wooded Boulder Clays, still awkward to traverse despite more extensive clearance, formed a barrier to this east—west trade and the area had, therefore, to produce its own goods.

The typical East Anglian pottery kiln was of the single stoke-hole updraught type with a circular firing chamber. It was constructed by excavating a cylindrical pit, lining it with clay and then placing a

74

clay pedestal in the centre of the chamber. This was connected to the walls by fire bars which supported the kiln floor. Pots were piled on the kiln floor and the chamber was covered by a domed roof, usually of turves, straw and clay built up on a framework of branches, with a smoke hole at the top. The roof would be broken down after each firing, but the base of the kiln was used a number of times. There are many variations in the details of Roman kilns (fig. 39), but this form is the commonest in East Anglia and continued in use until the end of the period.

At Grimstone End traces of huts were found associated with the kilns, and probably other potteries also incorporated living-quarters for the potters and their families. The types of pottery produced were local variants of the general Romano-British pot forms, and this industrialization of potting is a far cry from the local hand-made pots present in East Anglia during the Early Iron Age.

TOWNS: CAISTOR-BY-NORWICH

One of the features of the post-Boudiccan reorganization of East Anglia was the institution of a Romanized form of local administration which, in common with that of the rest of the country, was based on a system of *cantonal capitals,* that is, towns usually at the centre of the tribal areas. This resulted in the foundation of the first East Anglian town, Venta Icenorum (Caistor-by-Norwich), which lies on the River Tas, south-west of present-day Norwich. The town was founded about A.D. 70. A grid pattern of streets was laid out and surrounded by a bank and ditch. A lack of Romanization and great poverty after the Boudiccan revolt is suggested by the early buildings at Venta Icenorum which were built exclusively of wattle and daub, no doubt much in the same style as the traditional native rural buildings in the rest of East Anglia. No masonry buildings appeared in the town until the beginning of the second century when the Forum (market place at the centre of the town), Basilica (great hall) and a set of public baths were built. This building activity took place at the beginning of a period of prosperity, also evident in the development of villas in the countryside, when the drastic effects of the Boudiccan rebellion had finally been overcome and East Anglia was once more at peace. Even though the main public buildings were built in masonry during the first half of the second century the majority of the buildings in the town remained of wattle and daub, and they do not seem to have been replaced until later in the century, perhaps at the time when the town was encircled by a stout stone wall. This wall replaced earlier boundaries and, in fact, reduced by about one-fifth the area occupied by the town. The southern wall was built across the main north–south street (fig. 40), leaving part of that and its adjoining side streets beyond the wall's protection. This made the area of the town about 35 acres; either the original town plan had been found to be too large for the population, or the smaller area was more easily encircled by the walls.

The late second-century walls of Caistor-by-Norwich are interesting in that their outer faces were embellished by projecting towers, alternately rectangular and U-shaped; such features are not commonly found in the early defences of Roman towns in Britain. The purpose of the stone walls was probably to protect the town from occasional attack but,

75

Fig. 40 *Air view of Caistor-by-Norwich (Venta Icenorum)*

more expressly, to keep check on movements in and out of the gateways. The defences consisted of an external ditch, an internal earth bank, a stone wall eleven feet thick with tile bonding courses and four gates, one in each wall. The south gate was the most significant and consisted of an arched passageway flanked by guard houses. It was the point of entry into the town of the Roman road which ran from Colchester to Venta Icenorum, by way of the posting stations of Baylham House, Stoke Ash and Scole. In general the Roman roads of East

Anglia are little known and slightly investigated, but this road, the so-called Pye Road, is well attested and is probably yet another result of the administrative reorganization of East Anglia after the Boudiccan revolt.

The third century saw a good deal of activity at Venta, not all of it of a peaceful nature. The early years of the century witnessed new domestic buildings in the town but, by contrast, the Forum was allowed to lie in ruins from the beginning of the century until its reconstruction on a smaller and simpler plan about A.D. 270 Also in mid-century the bath-houses underwent considerable reconstruction and it may be that some civil disturbance or unrest led to the destruction of the town centre early in the century. A certain amount of inertia on the part of the citizens is indicated by their allowing the Forum to lie destroyed and derelict for so many years; this can also be seen in the fact that the guardrooms at the south gate were used as rubbish tips throughout the third century and were finally abandoned some time before A.D. 300, possibly a good deal earlier.

Occupation of Venta Icenorum continued throughout the fourth century, although in the latter half of the century barbarian federate soldiers had to be stationed there to protect the town from raids by the Saxon pirates of the North Sea. The fact that the troops were stationed in Venta indicates both that the town was particularly exposed to attack and that it was worth protecting; this may have been because of its function as a market and trading point for East Anglia—outside the walls remains of kilns attest a local pottery industry while glass making was also carried on. Perhaps the town's most important function was as the centre of the East Anglian wool trade, and much evidence has been produced for the presence of the woollen industry there—spindle whorls, loom weights, carding combs and larger weaving combs have all been found at Venta. Products from the town could be exported southwards down the Pye Road to Colchester, or along the rivers Tas and Wensum to Caister-by-Yarmouth which was developed as a trading port.

Despite the foreign garrison, occupation of Caistor-by-Norwich dwindled during the latter part of the fourth century and by about A.D. 400 some of the buildings had been destroyed by fire. It seems that the town ceased to be occupied during the fifth century, thereby suffering the same fate as many other Romano-British towns. The latest evidence from Venta comes from an Anglo-Saxon cemetery of about A.D. 450 outside its walls.

TOWNS: CAISTER-BY-YARMOUTH

The second town in East Anglia is Caister-by-Yarmouth, which was founded about A.D. 125, both as an outport for Caistor-by-Norwich and as a trading post between Roman Britain and the Low Countries. Its position commands the shortest sea crossing between England and the Rhine mouth, and its foundation coincided with the increasing import into England of Rhenish products—notably glass, pottery and millstones made of lava.

In its earliest phase the town was a rectangular area between 9 and 10 acres in extent, surrounded by a ditch, bank and wooden palisade (fig. 41). Then, during the second half of the second century, a stone wall with internal angle towers was built and this was followed by

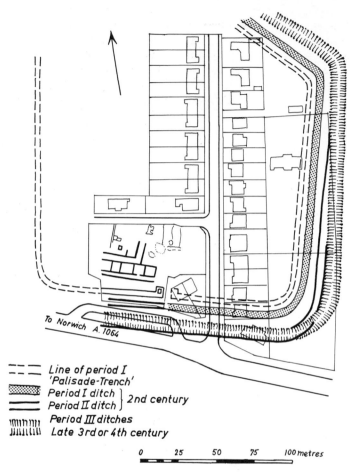

Line of period I
'Palisade-Trench'
Period I ditch ⎫
Period II ditch ⎬ 2nd century
Period III ditches
Late 3rd or 4th century

0   25   50   75   100 metres

Fig. 41 *Plan of the eastern part of Caister-by-Yarmouth*

greatly increased trading activity. A road ran down from the south gate of the town to the harbour, and just inside the south gate a large hostel or *mansio* for sailors was erected during the second century. This was repaired in the fourth century, and indicates that the town was still occupied and was probably fairly prosperous at that date.

Recent excavations have produced results which suggest that the town was originally founded as a military site during the second century and reverted to a purely civil role only at the beginning of the fourth century, when the Saxon Shore fort of Burgh Castle on the southern shore of Breydon Water took over the task of protecting Caister-by-

Yarmouth and the East Anglian interior; but whether this is so or not, it is certain that Caister-by-Yarmouth played an important part in trade from the second to the fourth centuries, and during the latter part of its history it was defended by the towering walls of Burgh Castle.

These two towns, Caistor-by-Norwich and Caister-by-Yarmouth, end the history of Roman urban development in East Anglia. Urbanization was much more successful in other parts of Roman Britain, especially in those areas where the pre-Roman Belgae had established large settlements in the first century B.C. and the first century A.D. This partly explains the success of Colchester, once the capital of the Catuvellauni; the Iceni, however, do not seem to have lived in large settlements or even in villages and were basically unsympathetic towards urban planning when it was introduced by the Romans.

THE MILITARY OCCUPATION OF EAST ANGLIA

The Boudiccan revolt of A.D. 61 can be taken as the starting point of the military aspect of Romanization in East Anglia. Once the rebellion had been quelled, temporary forts were established at strategic points; Great Chesterford on the River Cam was set up as a border fortress on the boundaries of the Iceni, and others were founded at Ixworth and Coddenham, both in Suffolk (the only remains of these forts are their plans revealed by air photography), and possibly also at Scole where the Pye Road crosses the River Waveney. In north Norfolk, Wighton Camp, a late first-century B.C. Icenian fortress, was reoccupied by the Romans a century later when the ditches were recut to the typical Roman V-shaped pattern. At nearby Thornham, also an Icenian settlement, the native huts were destroyed by fire and in their place a signal station was established, in such a position that beacons lit there could be seen across the Wash and summon help from the Roman army stationed in Lincolnshire.

Once they had played their part in the pacification of East Anglia the legions withdrew and most of the forts were allowed to decay. Thornham, however, was maintained during the second century and was probably refurbished at the time of the next emergency; but in general, East Anglia in the second and third centuries was essentially a non-military area with very little in the way of defences.

THE SAXON SHORE FORTS

The next phase of military building in East Anglia took place in the late third century when the presence of Saxon pirates in the English Channel and the North Sea caused the construction of the chain of fortresses around the east and south coasts of England known as the Forts of the Saxon Shore. In East Anglia three such forts were built, at Brancaster (Branodunum) on the north Norfolk coast, Burgh Castle (Gariannonum) at the mouth of the Waveney and the Yare, and Walton Castle near Felixstowe.

The main distinguishing characteristics of the Saxon Shore forts are their defences which are the result of third- and fourth-century adaptation of fort walls in response to the increasing use of the

simple, with cremation as the sole form of burial in the first century but giving way to inhumation by the third century.

Cremated bones were often placed in jars but sometimes they were buried in wooden boxes; the jars or boxes were generally placed in the ground without any form of surface mark, but occasionally they can be found inserted into an earlier burial, as in the Bronze Age barrow at Grimstone End in Suffolk, or, even more infrequently, within a barrow specifically constructed for the burial. Four Roman barrows are known from Rougham in Suffolk and one from Burnham Thorpe in Norfolk, and these are thought to represent intrusive customs from eastern Belgium. The number of known Roman cemeteries is small and their burial customs are not very distinctive; the Roman age is one of the few archaeological periods when we know more about the living population than the dead.

Romano-Celtic temples, in which a form of Roman and native pagan religion and ritual was practised, have been found at various sites in East Anglia. Outside the walls at Caistor-by-Norwich two temples were built in the early third century and near them an unusual Celtic finger ring (fig. 43) has recently been found and interpreted as an offering to the gods. At Whitedyke Farm, Hockwold, a circular timber-framed building, built in the early second century and in use until the late fourth century, contained ritual deposits of animal and bird bones buried beside the building's upright posts, and there were also a number of antler picks. Coins, fragments of bronze head-dresses and the hand from a bronze statuette were also found in the temple and, taken as a whole, the finds seem to indicate that the native population was continuing to worship in its own way but was influenced by the religion of the Classical gods.

When Christianity was made the official religion of the Roman Empire in the early fourth century it did little to stop the worship of heathen gods, and in East Anglia there is very little evidence for the early years of Christianity. The spoons from the Mildenhall treasure were embellished with Christian symbols and a cemetery at Ipswich may possibly have belonged to Roman Christians of the fourth century. This burial ground

Fig. 43 *Intaglio of a ring decorated with three heads in profile, from Caistor-by-Norwich*

82

contained rows of graves which were all inhumations without grave goods and with the skeletons orientated east–west. In contrast, at Mundford in Norfolk, a fourth-century inhumation continued the pagan practice of depositing grave goods with burials and a fourth-century brooch, a strap-end and a worn mid-fourth-century coin were found in the grave.

THE END OF THE ROMAN AGE

There is much evidence to show that life was very unsettled in Britain during the latter part of Roman rule, particularly in the fourth century. There were many signs of weakness on the part of the Roman administrative, defensive and economic systems and from the middle of the fourth century onwards the decline of Roman Britain became very pronounced.

One of the most traumatic shocks came in A.D. 367 when England was invaded by Picts, Scots and Saxons, much of the countryside ravaged and many towns attacked. The country was soon restored to order, however, by the efforts of Count (later Emperor) Theodosius who, in about A.D. 369, restored and modernized the walls of many towns along the lines of the defences of the Saxon Shore forts and took the dangerous step of garrisoning some of them, as for instance Caistor-by-Norwich, with Germanic auxiliary soldiers. In this way the Romans themselves took the initiative in settling the Anglo-Saxons permanently on English soil; before that time the raiders and pirates had made brief forays into the country and then retired to their homeland. The federate troops remained as a threatening presence throughout the rest of the fourth

century and even in the early years of the fifth century.

One of the results of barbarian presence on Romano-British soil was the development of a specific type of pottery designed to conform to their tastes in decoration; this is generally known as *Romano-Saxon pottery* and was made during the latter part of the fourth century. This pottery seems to have been produced by the normal Romano-British potteries in the most common red or grey fabrics, but it differs from its purely Romano-British counterparts in that the style and decoration of the wares are almost entirely Anglo-Saxon (fig. 44). The distribution of this hybrid type is con-

Fig. 44 *Romano-Saxon pottery from Icklingham and Lakenheath*

83

fined to the eastern half of England and is concentrated in the Saxon Shore forts and their immediate vicinity. In East Anglia most Romano-Saxon pottery has come from Burgh Castle, its neighbouring civilian port of Caister-by-Yarmouth and from the cantonal capital, Caistor-by-Norwich. We know that Burgh Castle and Caistor-by-Norwich were defended by *foederati* in the fourth century and it is reasonable to assume that Caister-by-Yarmouth was also defended in this way. Similar pottery has also been found at Brundall and West Acre in Norfolk, and Icklingham and Lakenheath in Suffolk, usually close beside Roman roads or other means of communication. Romano-Saxon wares are one of the earliest signs of Saxon taste in this country, but they seem to die out at the beginning of the fifth century when the Roman potteries began to go out of production and pottery was once again made by hand.

It seems that by about 400 A.D. the Anglo-Saxon mercenaries and Romano-British civilians were co-operating to keep the peace and defend the country from attack from outside. But this state of equilibrium did not last long as the Roman Empire began to break up and the Roman troops withdrew. The first sign of economic disruption was shown by the decline in the amount of currency in circulation; this began during the reign of Emperor Theodosius and after A.D. 407 no new coins were issued. From that time onwards coins were more often hoarded than used as currency and by about A.D. 430 monetary economy in Roman Britain had collapsed altogether. Similarly, once the Roman troops withdrew and official connections with Rome were cut off in A.D. 410, industries in Roman Britain declined and the decade from A.D. 410 saw the end of such large-scale concerns as the potteries. Villas decayed along with the economy and, although some towns at least were occupied throughout the first half of the fifth century, it was only by employing foreign mercenaries as their protectors that they managed to survive.

East Anglia was affected by this decline as much as any other part of Roman Britain and was one of the first areas to be settled permanently by Anglo-Saxon farmers. Once the region had settled down to Anglo-Saxon rule it began to flourish once more, and the 1000 years from the arrival of the Anglo-Saxons to the end of the Middle Ages saw East Anglia becoming a prosperous and highly populous region, far richer materially and culturally than it had ever been in prehistoric and Roman times.

Sites to Visit

Because of the nature of the landscape and the type of building materials available East Anglia is not rich in prehistoric or Roman remains which have left traces on the ground, but the following list gives a number of monuments where some remains have been preserved. Where a site is in the care of the Ministry of Public Building and Works this has been mentioned; the rest stand either on common land or in private grounds but are generally accessible by means of footpaths.

NORFOLK

ARMINGHALL

HENGE MONUMENT
DATE: Neolithic
MAP REF.: TG 240060
DIRECTIONS: On the west side of the minor road running from Trowse Newton (on A146) to Caistor St. Edmund.
Greatly destroyed through ploughing and cultivation but traces of the banks can still be seen.
Chapter Four; *Proceedings of the Prehistoric Society* II, 1936

CAISTER-BY-YARMOUTH

ROMAN TOWN
DATE: Second to fifth centuries
MAP REF.: TG 518125
DIRECTIONS: In the area formed by the junction of the roads A149 and A1064, west of Caister-on-Sea.
Some remains of the walls and town buildings exposed through excavation.
Chapter Seven; *Norfolk Archaeology* XXXIV, 1963; Ministry of Public Building and Works

CAISTOR-BY-NORWICH

ROMAN TOWN
DATE: First to fifth centuries
MAP REF.: TG 230035

DIRECTIONS: To west of a minor road, half a mile south of Caistor St. Edmund. Parish church stands in one corner of the town area. Remains of the defences can be seen.
Chapter Seven; *Archaeological J.* CVI, 1949

HOLKHAM

FORT
DATE: Iron Age
MAP REF.: TF 875446
DIRECTIONS: North of A149, one mile west of Holkham village. Accessible by track over marshes.
Defences can be seen.
Chapter Six; *Archaeological J.* XCVI, 1940

NARBOROUGH

FORT
DATE: Iron Age
MAP REF.: TF 751130
DIRECTIONS: North-east of Narborough village on A47.
Remains of defences, but very heavily wooded.
Chapter Six; *Archaeological J.* XCVI, 1940

SALTHOUSE

ROUND BARROWS
DATE: Bronze Age
MAP REF.: TG 069421
DIRECTIONS: On Salthouse Heath, high ground two miles south of Salthouse village on A149.
Large group of barrows on open heathland.

TASBURGH

FORT
DATE: Iron Age
MAP REF.: TM 200960
DIRECTIONS: On the minor road between Tasburgh and Upper Tasburgh.
Slight traces of defences.
Chapter Six; *Archaeological J.* XCVI, 1940

THETFORD

FORT
DATE: Iron Age
MAP REF.: TL 875828
DIRECTIONS: In south-east quarter of town.
Part of the Iron Age fort remains although
obscured by the earthworks of the Norman
castle.
Chapter Six

WARHAM

FORT
DATE: Iron Age
MAP REF.: TF 945408
DIRECTIONS: One mile north of Wighton.
Approached by trackway from minor road.
Best preserved of the East Anglian forts.
Double rampart and ditch enclose an almost
circular area of about three and a half acres.
The south-west side partly destroyed by the
River Stiffkey.
Chapter Six; *Antiquaries J.* XXXIII, 1933

WEETING

GRIMES GRAVES FLINT MINES
DATE: Neolithic
MAP REF.: TL 816898
DIRECTIONS: In Thetford Chase. Two miles
south of B1108, four miles north-east of
Brandon.
Several of the mine shafts are open to the
public.
Chapter Four; Ministry of Public Building
and Works *Guidebook*

WEST RUDHAM

LONG BARROW
DATE: Neolithic
MAP REF.: TF 810253
DIRECTIONS: At the west end of West
Rudham Common, one and a half miles
south-east of Harpley.
Remains of long barrow; rare in East
Anglia.
Chapter Four; *Norfolk Archaeology*
XXVII, 1940

SUFFOLK

BURGH CASTLE

SAXON SHORE FORT
DATE: Third and fourth centuries
MAP REF.: TG 475046
DIRECTIONS: At the west end of Burgh
Castle village, south of the church.
Defensive walls, still standing to a height
of 15 feet in places.
Chapter Seven; Ministry of Public Building
and Works *Guidebook*

CLARE CAMP

FORT
DATE: Iron Age
MAP REF.: TL 769458
DIRECTIONS: North of the village of Clare,
on west side of B1063.
Remains of double rampart and ditch.
Chapter Six; *Archaeological J.* XCVI, 1940

Museums to Visit

The following museums contain collections of prehistoric and Roman material from East
Anglia:

BURY ST. EDMUNDS	*Moyse's Hall Museum, Cornhill*
CAMBRIDGE	*University Museum of Archaeology and Ethnology, Downing Street*
COLCHESTER	*Colchester and Essex Museum, The Castle*
FRAMLINGHAM	*Museum of the Framlingham and District Local History and Preservation Society*

GREAT YARMOUTH	*Tolhouse Museum, Tolhouse Street*
IPSWICH	*The Museum, High Street*
KING'S LYNN	*The Museum and Art Gallery, Market Street*
LONDON	*The British Museum*
MILDENHALL	*Museum of the Mildenhall Natural History and Archaeological Society*
NORWICH	*The Castle Museum*
OXFORD	*The Ashmolean Museum*
SANDRINGHAM	*The Estate Museum*
SOUTHWOLD	*The Museum, St. Bart's Green*
THETFORD	*Ancient House Museum*
WISBECH	*Wisbech and Fenland Museum*

A List of Books

ABBREVIATIONS:
Antiq. J.   The Antiquaries Journal
NA   Norfolk Archaeology
PCAS   Proceedings of the Cambridge Antiquarian Society
PPS   Proceedings of the Prehistoric Society
PSIA   Proceedings of the Suffolk Institute of Archaeology

GENERAL

C. Fox, *The Archaeology of the Cambridge Region*, 1923.
R. R. Clarke, *East Anglia*, 1960.
H. Godwin, *The History of the British Flora*, 1956.
C. P. Chatwin, *British Regional Geology, East Anglia and Adjoining Areas*, 4th ed., 1961.
British Association for the Advancement of Science, *Norwich and its Region*, 1961.

PALAEOLITHIC PERIOD

J. M. Coles, 'Ancient Man in Europe', in J. M. Coles and D. D. A. Simpson (eds.), *Studies in Ancient Europe*, 1968.
J. M. Coles and E. S. Higgs, *The Archaeology of Early Man*, 1969.
J. Wymer, *Lower Palaeolithic Archaeology in Britain*, 1968.

MESOLITHIC PERIOD

J. G. D. Clark, *The Mesolithic Age in Britain*, 1932.
J. E. Sainty, 'Mesolithic Sites in Norfolk', *NA* XXVIII, 1945.
J. G. D. Clark, 'A Microlithic Industry from the Cambridgeshire Fenland and Other Industries of Sauveterrian Affinities from Britain', *PPS* XXI, 1955.

NEOLITHIC PERIOD

J. G. D. Clark et al., 'Excavations at the Neolithic Site at Hurst Fen, Mildenhall, Suffolk, 1954, 1957 and 1958', *PPS* XXVI, 1960.

J. G. D. Clark and H. Godwin, 'The Neolithic in the Cambridgeshire Fens', *Antiquity* XXXVI, 141, 1962.

J. G. D. Clark, 'Radiocarbon Dating and the Expansion of Farming Culture from the Near East over Europe', *PPS* XXXI, 1965.

A. H. A. Hogg, 'A Long Barrow at West Rudham, Norfolk', *NA* XXVII, 1941.

BRONZE AGE

J. G. D. Clark, 'Report on a Late Bronze Age Site in Mildenhall Fen, West Suffolk', *Antiq. J.* XVI, 1936.

T. C. Kelly, 'A Series of Late Middle Bronze Age Sites, Wilde Street, Mildenhall', *PSIA* XXXI, Pt. 1, 1967.

G. Briscoe, 'Swales Tumulus: A Combined Neolithic A and Bronze Age Barrow at Worlington, Suffolk', *PCAS* L, 1957.

N. Smedley and E. Owles, 'Pottery of the Early and Early Middle Bronze Age in Suffolk', *PSIA* XXIX, 1962.

C. F. C. Hawkes and R. R. Clarke, 'Gahlstorf and Caister-on-Sea', in I. Ll. Foster and L. Alcock (eds.), *Culture and Environment*, 1963.

B. A. V. Trump, 'Fenland Rapiers', in J. M. Coles and D. D. A. Simpson (eds.), *Studies in Ancient Europe*, 1968.

IRON AGE

B. Cunliffe, 'Early Pre-Roman Iron Age Communities in Eastern England', *Antiq. J.* XLVIII, Pt. II, 1968.

J. G. D. Clark and C. I. Fell, 'The Early Iron Age Site at Micklemoor Hill, West Harling, Norfolk, and its Pottery', *PPS* XIX, 1953.

C. Fox, *Pattern and Purpose*, 1958.

R. R. Clarke, 'The Early Iron Age Treasure from Snettisham, Norfolk', *PPS* XX. 1954.

E. Owles, 'The Ipswich Gold Torcs', *Antiquity* XLIII, 171, 1969.

E. Owles and N. Smedley, 'Two Belgic Cemeteries at Boxford', *PSIA* XXXI, Pt. 1, 1967.

Ordnance Survey, *Map of Southern Britain in the Iron Age*, 1962.

ROMAN PERIOD

J. W. Brailsford, *The Mildenhall Treasure—a Handbook*, 1955.

C. A. Peal, 'Romano-British Pewter Plates and Dishes', *PCAS* LX, 1967.

K. S. Painter, 'A Roman Bronze Helmet from Hawkedon', *PSIA* XXXI, Pt. 1, 1967.

S. J. Hallam, 'Villages in Roman Britain: Some Evidence', *Antiq. J.* XLIV, 1964.

P. Salway, 'Excavations at Hockwold-cum-Wilton, Norfolk, 1961–2', *PCAS* LX, 1967.

J. A. Ellison, 'Excavations at Caister-on-Sea, 1962–3', *NA* XXXIV, Pt. 1, 1963.

R. F. Tylecote and E. Owles, 'A Second Century Iron Smelting Site at Ashwicken, Norfolk', *NA* XXXII, 1961.

S. E. West, 'Romano-British Pottery Kilns on West Stow Heath', *PSIA* XXVI, 1952.

Ordnance Survey, *Map of Roman Britain*, 1956.

S. S. Frere, *Britannia*, 1967.

Index

90